IMMIGRATION, THE PUBLIC SCHOOL, AND THE 20TH CENTURY AMERICAN ETHOS

The Jewish Immigrant As a Case Study

Alan Wieder

UNIVERSITY
PRESS OF
AMERICA

LANHAM • NEW YORK • LONDON

Copyright © 1985 by

University Press of America,® Inc.

4720 Boston Way
Lanham. MD 20706

3 Henrietta Street
London WC2E 8LU England

Library of Congress Cataloging-in-Publication Data

Wieder, Alan, 1949-
  Immigration, the public school, and the 20th century
American ethos.

  Bibliography: p.
  1. Jews—United States—Cultural assimilation.
2. United States—Emigration and immigration.
3. Public schools—United States—History—20th
century. I. Title.
E184.J5W52   1985   305.8'924'073   85-11263
ISBN 0-8191-4793-1 (alk. paper)
ISBN 0-8191-4794-X (pbk. : alk. paper)

All University Press of America books are produced on acid-free
paper which exceeds the minimum standards set by the National
Historical Publications and Records Commission.

DEDICATION

    To my grandmother, Sylvia Shapiro, who made the immigrant journey and to my teacher, Bernard Mehl, who is able to wed Yiddishkite and Academia.

TABLE OF CONTENTS

CHAPTER 1

INTRODUCTION: THE 20TH CENTURY AMERICAN ETHOS

Kierkegaard and Nietzche were nineteenth century men, yet each foresaw the dangers of twentieth century mass society. The atomization that comes with mass man was predicted in The Present Age and The Gay Science. In The Present Age, Kierkegaard describes the leveling process of mass society. Every man is the same and there is no way to distinguish between justice and injustice--between friend or enemy--there are no friends.[1] Nietzche saw it as a trade off:

> If you decide for the former and desire to diminish and lower the level of human pain, you also have to diminish and lower the level of their capacity for joy. Actually science can promote either goal. So far it may still be better known for its power of depriving man of his joys and making him colder, more like a statue, more stoic.[2]

Discussion and analysis of alienation and fragmentation are found in the work of Jaques Ellul, Paul Goodman, and Mary and Lester Josephson. Ellul in The Technological Society discusses the mechanization of modern man.[3] For Ellul, man created technique and is now just a tool of his own creation. To be for or against the machine is unimportant because mass man is part of that very machine.[4] In fact, for Ellul, to be against anything is abstract because there are only impersonal acts. Whether it is work, play, art, or love we act according to technique. There can be no personal involvement.[5]

> It is impossible to make industrial labor interesting by allowing the worker to introduce his own personality into it. He must be rendered completely unconscious and mechanized in such a way that he cannot even dream of asserting himself. The technical problem is to make his gestures so automatic that they have no personal quality at all.[6]

For Ellul, mass man's acts are controlled and contrived; it is the ultimate impersonalism because man acts as his own controller.

Growing Up Absurd by Paul Goodman talks of youth having no place in American society.[7] He talks of kids

1

not being able to find work and that when they do the job does not make any sense. One example is of a boy getting a job as a mechanic and then finding out that he was not supposed to fix cars:

> He then learns that the cars have built-in obsolescence, that the manufacturers do not want them to be repaired or repairable? They have lobbied a law that requires them to provide spare parts for only five years (it used to be ten). Repairing the new cars is often a matter of cosmetics not mechanics; and the repairs are pointlessly expensive . . . Gone are the days of keeping the jalopies in good shape, the artist-work of a proud mechanic.[8]

This is just one example that Goodman makes as he speaks of the lack of community, the lack of trust, and the lack of faith in American young people. For Goodman the alienation of youth makes sense and Growing Up Absurd calls for a worthwhile and sensible world:

> My purpose is a simple one: to show how it is desperately hard these days for an average child to grow up to be a man, for our present organized system of society does not want men. They are not safe. They do not suit.[10]

The Josephsons in their book Man Alone discuss the history of alienation with the conclusion that modern man suffers from his own unique strand.[11] Throughout history man has been alienated but that alienation was because of nature rather than his fellow man. There was a place for man in the tribe or community and the threat of alienation came from the outside. He felt small, but it was in his relationship with the world. He still was in touch with his brother and his work. Modern man now beats nature but finds himself more isolated and alone than tribal man:

> Knowledge has spread, but it has not abolished war, or fear; nor has it made all men brothers. Instead, men find themselves more isolated, anxious and uneasy than ever.[12]

There is also a positive side to mass society. Economic progress and greater human equality are part of twentieth century America. Eric Goldman discusses

each in Rendezvous With Destiny. Government acts as
well as human aspirations and progress are included in
Goldman's study.[13] Rendezvous With Destiny is a book
that tells us of the great number of liberal reforms
and government initiated projects that serve American
society. Bureaucracy and impersonalism are not denied
but the high standard of living because of government
works is stressed in Goldman's book. The positive
aspects of mass society are also discussed in The
School and Society by John Dewey. He discusses the
tremendous educational opportunities and possibilities
for American youth:[14]

> The result has been an intellectual
> revolution. Learning has been put into
> circulation. While there still is, and
> probably always will be a particular class
> having the special business of inquiry in
> hand, a distinctively learned class is
> henceforth out of the question. It is an
> anachronism. Knowledge is no longer an
> immobile solid; it has been liquefied. It is
> actively moving in all the currents of
> society itself.[15]

Modern technological progress cannot be "given
back". At the same time, alienation and fragmentation
are part of the condition of modern man. Numerous
books on loneliness cross discipline lines; their
existence cannot be denied. In Classical Educational
Ideas, Bernard Mehl denies neither our progress nor our
imperonalism but instead asks for the realization of
human limits.

> The answer to impersonalism is not to
> deny the quest for well being. A
> back-to-nature movement is not in the cards.
> To suffer the plight of those who are close
> to nature comes to role-playing, while those
> who were there--Hawaiians, American
> Indians--were killed by syphilis and scarlet
> fever. We cannot be Eskimos or head hunters,
> Thoreau to the contrary. There is no exit
> for modern affluent man except through the
> establishment of limits to the goal of well
> being.[16]

Much has been written on the connection between
fragmented society and the American dream. A major
focus of this study is to better understand the
elements that connect progress and equality with

3

alienation and fragmentation. Professor Mehl seems to be right when he speaks of "limits". It is this sense of limits that helps to shape this study. Can progress and equality come in a world which is not impersonal? Or is impersonalism the price we choose to pay for progress and equality? This tension might be better understood with greater understanding of ethnicity and the "American dream".

The sociologist Will Herberg, and Jeffrey Herold of Ohio State University have done work on this topic. Herberg's book, Protestant--Catholic--Jew, examines the growing number of similarities and the lessening number of differences of religious sects in American society.[17] For Herberg, there was a time when religion was a divisive force, but that is less and less the case in twentieth century America.[18] Since there is little difference between sects, we are able to get along in what he calls the "American way".

> Religious groupings throughout American society have been stamped with recognizably American qualities, to an extent indeed where foreign observers sometimes find the various American religions more like each other than they are like their European counterparts.[19]

Herberg is not for or against the new type of religion which he describes, but he warns of the danger of inauthenticity that accompanies the secularization of religion. "The witness to authentic Jewish-Christian faith may well prove much more difficult under these conditions than when faith has to contend with overt and avowed unbelief."[20] He still cannot help but be impressed by Protestant, Jew, and Catholic coming together in twentieth century America for interfaith activity. Herberg wants to be convinced that the breakdown of religious differences brings man closer to his fellow man, but he still holds reservations.

Jeffrey Herold's dissertation, The American Faith in the Schools As An Agency of Progress: Promise and Fulfillment, examines the public school as the American church. One chapter is even titled, "The School as the American National Church". Herold examines our faith in education as a means of social and economic mobility.[21] The school is a means to end diversity, including ethnicity, and in so doing people come together as Americans, both socially and economically.[22] Herold tells us of the immigrant's belief in the schools as the procurer of the "American

4

dream," and the end of social and economic barriers, one of which was ethnicity.[23]

For this writer, the thesis that ethnicity is a cause of atomization and the breakdown of ethnicity through the "American dream" is a cause of communion is invalid. There is no question that ethnicity involves diverse groups. However, it is hypothesized that in those diverse groups lie the roots that nourish the possibilities of communion rather than atomization. In the book <u>Anti-Semite and Jew</u>, Jean-Paul Sartre says that the Jew who is more Jewish will have greater communion with his fellow man.[24] For Sartre the breaking down of ethnicity leaves man suspended and part of nothing. Being part of nothing, he is inauthentic and there is no possiblity for communion. Sartre tells us that there are two types of Anti-Semitism. The first type is the common thesis of bigotry against the man because he is Jewish.[25] The second type is getting rid of the man's Jewishness and then you can treat him as a man.[26] But for Sartre, treating the Jew as a man and not as a Jew is an impossibility:

> But the man does not exist; there are Jews, Protestants, Catholics; there are Frenchmen, Englishmen, Germans. There are whites, blacks, yellows. In short, these drastic measures of coercion would mean the annihilation of a spiritual community, founded on custom and affection, to the advantage of the national community. Most conscious Jews would refuse assimilation if it were presented to them under this aspect. Certainly they wish to integrate themselves in the nation, but as Jews.[27]

Sartre continues by explaining the possibility of real communion. He calls it "concrete liberalism".

> Jews--and likewise the Arabs and the Negroes--from the moment that they are participants in the national enterprise, have a right in that enterprise; they are citizens. But they have these rights as Jews, negroes, or Arabs--that is, as concrete persons.[28]

Sartre's liberal concept asks serious questions of the liberal ideas reviewed above. It might be that the breaking down of ethnicity is part of twentieth century alienation and fragmentation rather than the beginnings of greater communion of man with his fellow man. It is with this possibility in mind that this study of American ethnicity is undertaken. It is to the ethnics that it turns first because twentieth century America is the Jew, the Pole, the Italian, the Black, and others. It is in this ethnicity that American roots lie.

It is the twofold purpose of this study: (1) to trace the progress of the early twentieth century Jewish immigrant so that we might better understand the mass society in which we live, and (2) to explicate certain of the most important implications of this historical context for contemporary education.

The report of the study is divided into three chapters and a conclusion which discuss the immigrant and the public school. The eastern European Jewish immigrant is used to exemplify this journey of "becoming American". It is in his becoming American, it is his dealings with the public school and society in general that we might better understand what C. Wright Mills calls the twentieth century American ethos. The following are the three questions that are asked throughout the book:

1. Are the "American dream" and "melting pot" concepts myth or reality?

2. Did the public school help or in fact harm immigrant children?

3. What is the relationship between the public school and alienation and fragmentation?

Chapter 2 is divided into three parts. Alienation and fragmentation as discussed by Mills opens the chapter. For Mills, it is a choice that Americans opt for when they choose "progress".[29] The second part of the chapter is an example of Mills' thesis. The Jewish immigrant is studied as he becomes American. Three facets of immigrant life are studied as they changed from the time of immigration. The house of worship, the family, and the occupations of the Jewish immigrants trace the many changes in Jewish life as the Jew became American. Irving Howe's book, World of Our Fathers, as well as the work of Abraham Cahan, longtime editor of the Jewish Daily Forward, and Yiddish author Isaac Bashevis Singer served as sources for this section. Jewish life in the shtetl (a small

6

self-contained community) of eastern Europe and Jewish
life in New York City were like lives in different
worlds. Included in the Jewish immigrant experience
are the concepts of the American dream and the melting
pot. Discussion of these concepts conclude the second
chapter. Moynihan and Glazer argued them as myth while
Oscar Handlin discussed the reality of both concepts
for the immigrant American. It is this argument that
leads to Chapter 3 and the public school.

Chapter 3 reviews the literature written about the
schooling of the immigrant. Both sides of question two
are discussed. Did the school open things up or was it
a means of keeping people in their place? This chapter
traces the literature to analyze alternative positions
with respect to these questions. The review of
literature is divided into five parts. First, there
are those who laud the public school. Included are
educational historian, Ellwood Cubberley and early
twentieth century Boston school superintendent, Frank
V. Thompson. Then, there is a group who has been
labeled "the revisionists". They outline the evils of
public schooling for the immigrant children. This
group includes Colin Greer, Michael Katz, Paul Violas,
and Clarence Karier. Henry Perkinson, Lawrence Cremin,
and David Tyack follow the revisionists. They do not
deny the problems in the schooling of the immigrant,
but at the same time, they do not see the school as the
"killer" of immigrant children. Mark Krug, Maxine
Seller, and Timothy Smith add literature that deals
specifically with the melting pot idea and the
schooling of the immigrant. The chapter concludes with
two American dream stories. Leonard Covello and Mary
Antin sing praise to the public school. But neither
their testimony nor the harsh criticism of the
revisionists really brought answers to our questions.
The inconclusiveness of the literature suggests that
one way to come closer to the problem being studied is
through the recording of the memories of people who
immigrated and attended the public school. There are
obvious limitations involved in this approach to
history which should be noted at the outset. The
perils of memory and the possibility of cliche-ridden
interviews exists. Also there is the possibility of
the "halo effect" for the people interviewed. However,
oral history is defended here as the most reasonable
historical method.[30] Chapter 4 demonstrates this
alternative.

The text of Chapter 4 is clearly oral history. A
discussion of the discipline of oral history opens the

chapter. The strengths and the weaknesses of the discipline are examined. The widespread recognition of Alex Haley's work is a case in point. Although Haley's Roots is not history in a "pure" sense, his oral methodology has given the field added popularity and validity. In the final analysis, oral history addresses the lives of every man. We are part of living history and our lives have just as much historical validity as the lives of the duke and the duchess. In a sense, it is a choice for history being and touching the common man. One man who believes in the common man as history is Chicago journalist Studs Terkel. It is Terkel who has made such interviews famous. His books--Hard Times, Division Street America, Working, and American Dreams Lost and Found--make the times very real through the lives of the people he interviews. From his work came the approach taken in this investigation, namely the interviewing of Jewish immigrants who attended the public school. Terkel believes that history resides in real, everyday people and his view of history makes sense. Who should know what happened in the public school better than the people who were there? From over thirty interviews with Jewish immigrants in Cleveland, Ohio, thirteen, judged to be the most prototypical, are summarized in this chapter. Their public school memories, their occupations, and the lives of their children and their grandchildren are reported. Their public school memories acquaint us with everyday school occurrences. Teachers and courses are remembered so that we get a picture of life in the public school. Home life and religion are discussed in the context of their relationship to the school. In the occupations of the immigrants we see the differences between their work and the work of their fathers. This is extended as we study the second and third generations. With those generations we begin to see social, economic, and locational mobility. The chapter concludes with a charting of educational, occupational, and locational geneology.

It is from the lives of the people interviewed as well as from an analysis of the literature that alternative answers to the questions posed begin to evolve. The trends that appear in the interviews not only suggest answers to the questions, but they also identify leads for further questions.

Footnotes

[1]Soren Kierkegaard, _The Present Age_ (New York: Harper and Row, 1962), pp. 54-55.

[2]Friedrich Nietzche, _The Gay Science_ (New York): Vintage, 1974), p. 86.

[3]Jaques Ellul, _The Technological Society_ (New York: Knopf Inc., 1964), p. 334.

[4]Ibid.

[5]Ibid., pp. 387-399.

[6]Ibid., p. 399.

[7]Paul Goodman, _Growing Up Absurd_ (New York: Random House, 1960), pp. 17-52.

[8]Ibid., pp. 17-18.

[9]Ibid., p. 14.

[10]Ibid.

[11]Mary and Lester Josephson, _Man Alone_ (New York: Dell, 1962), p. 10.

[12]Ibid.

[13]Eric Goldman, _Rendezvous With Destiny_ (New York: Alfred A. Knopf, 1956), pp. 103-146.

[14]John Dewey, _The School and Society_ (Chicago: University of Chicago Press, 1943), pp. 24-25.

[15]Ibid.

[16]Bernard Mehl, _Classic Educational Ideas_ (Columbus, Ohio: Merrill Publishing, 1972), pp. 211-212.

[17]Will Herberg, _Protestant--Catholic--Jew_ (New York: Doubleday, 1955), pp. 247-270.

[18]Ibid., pp. 85-104.

[19]Ibid., p. 95.

[20]Ibid., p. 288.

[21]Jeffrey Herold, The American Faith in the Schools An Agency of Progress: Promise and Fulfillment (unpublished Ph.D. dissertaion, The Ohio State University, 1969), pp. 219-332.

[22]Ibid.

[23]Ibid., pp. 128-129.

[24]Jean-Paul Sartre, Anti-Semite and Jew (New York: Schocken Books, 1965), pp. 136-137.

[25]Ibid., p. 15.

[26]Ibid., pp. 55-58.

[27]Ibid., pp. 144-145.

[28]Ibid., p. 146.

[29]C. Wright Mills, White Collar (New York: Oxford University Press, 1956), p. xiii.

[30]See the first section of Karl Mannheim, Ideology and Utopia (New York: International Library of Psychology, 1936). His sociology of knowledge argument applies to this study. Oral History does not stand outside of but rather runs concurrently with the other methodology in the discipline. It undergoes the same scrutiny and is to be used with documents, letters, modern day cliometrics, etc. The purpose of this study is not to deny the others but the study does affirm the place of oral history within the discipline.

CHAPTER 2

THE IMMIGRANT EXPERIENCE--PROGRESS AND ATOMIZATION

In Power, Politics, and People, C. Wright Mills
discusses the rootlessness historically inherent in the
American ethos. He claims that there is no tradition
because there is nothing to derive tradition from. For
Mills, we left whatever we had of tradition for a
"middle class liberal ethic".[1] The middle class had to
deny tradition because it was always moving, changing,
and progressing. Mills discussed twentieth century
American rootlessness at greater length in White
Collar. He speaks of the middle class as "little men"
who choose this route in order to get ahead.

> The new Little Man seems to have no firm
> roots, no sure loyalties to sustain his life
> and give it a center. He is not aware of
> having any history, his past being as brief
> as it is unheroic; he has lived through no
> golden age he can recall in time of trouble.
> Perhaps because he does not know where he is
> going, he is in a frantic hurry; perhaps
> because he does not know what frightens him,
> he is paralyzed with fear.   This is
> especially a feature of his political life,
> where the paralysis results in the most
> profound apathy of modern times.[2]

Mills continues, saying that rootlessness envelops
our times.

> The uneasiness, the malaise of our time,
> is due to this root fact: in our politics
> and economy, in family life and religion--in
> practically   every   sphere   of   our
> existence--the certainties of the eighteenth
> and nineteenth centuries have disintegrated
> or been destroyed and, at the same time, no
> new sanctions or justifications for the new
> routines we live, and must live, have taken
> hold. So there is no acceptance and there is
> no rejection, no sweeping hope and no
> rebellion. There is no plan of life. Among
> white collar people the malaise is deep
> rooted; for the absence of any order of
> belief has left them morally defenseless as
> individuals and politically impotent as a
> group. Newly created in a harsh time of
> creation, white collar man has no culture to

11

lean upon except the contents of mass society that has shaped him and seeks to manipulate him to its alien ends. For security's sake he must strain to attach himself somewhere, but no communities or organizations seem to be thoroughly his.[3]

Mills explains that the European immigrant was willing to leave tradition behind in favor of progress. He believed in the American dream and he wanted a piece of the action.

> For two generations sons and daughters of the poor have looked forward eagerly to becoming even 'mere' clerks. Parents have sacrificed to have even one child finish high school, business school, or college so that he could be the assistant to the executive, do the filing, type the letter, teach school, work in the government office, do something requiring technical skills; hold a white collar job.[4]

The late nineteenth and early twentieth century brought many eastern European Jews, as well as Slavs, and Italians, to the United States. This is referred to as the wave of "new immigration". The new immigrants were not Nordic people as the old immigrants had been and they were looked at as being different than earlier immigrants and native Americans.[5] In a book titled A History of American Immigration, written in 1926, Professor George M. Stephenson says that the fear of the new immigrant is unfounded and trite. One thing that cannot be denied is that great numbers of new immigrants came to this country. Italian immigration was at its height between 1900 and 1916.[6] Jewish immigration was greater than ever before; a million and a half Jews came from Europe between 1880 and 1910. Of these over a million came from Russia and the rest came from Rumania and Austria-Hungary.[7] The Slavs also came in great numbers beginning in the 1880's. Twenty to thirty thousand came annually and the numbers increased greatly at the turn of the century. One hundred twenty thousand Slavs immigrated to America in 1903 which was the peak year.[8]

> Political and religious oppression and adventure cannot be denied as contributing factors, but emigration from Europe to America was often an economic decision. For many of the immigrants the reasons cannot be separated. Economic depression was a result

12

of religious and political problems. Carlos Levi, in his novel Christ Stopped at Eboli, tells us of Sicilian peasants being lured by what was for them great sums of money to work on construction gangs in America.[9] Oftentimes the money the immigrant was to be paid for his work was late or never. He was hired help and middlemen called padroni chipped away at his already meager wages. Levi goes on to talk of the breakdown of peasant life and the opportunity America presented for the Italian peasant. The small amount of money the immigrant made was like a great fortune back in Italy. Many people traveled back and forth and the emigrant was treated like a nobleman upon his return. The return trips eventually ceased and before long the Italian immigrant was American.[10] As good as this country was for the immigrant, life was not easy and he often felt very much alone in his new land. But immigrant letters sent back to Europe seldom mirrored the loneliness the immigrant felt. To the contrary he wrote home about the great opportunity and often urged his friends to join him in the land of milk and honey. This is the conclusion of a letter written by a Swedish immigrant:

> Whoever wants to work can get ahead in America. It is a good country and has been a support to many poor people, both from Sweden and elsewhere.[11]

In the literature that alludes to letters the content mentioned does not differ from this example. In a book called The Immigrant, written in 1913 by Frederick Haskin, the author claims that the letters written to Europe was one of the reasons for the influx of immigration.[12]

Whatever the reason, coming to America denies what it is to be a peasant. There was a time when the peasant would not have left the land no matter what the prize. Leaving meant that what he was once a part of was now over.

> Emigration was the end of peasant life in Europe; it was also the beginning of life in America . . . All the new conditions had conspired to depress the peasants into a hopeless mass, to take away their distinguishing differences and to deprive them, to an ever-greater extent of the capacity for making willful decisions.[13]

13

Whether it be the Italian peasant or eastern European Jew, one thing remains constant. For each group something was over and immigration to America was the beginning of something new.

The leaving of the old for the new is exemplified well in the move of the Jews from the eastern European shtetl to the American suburb. The shtetl of eastern Europe and the Jewish suburbs of New Rochelle, New York, or Beachwood, Ohio, have little, if anything, in common. Dostoyevsky's "If God is dead then all is possible"[14] might be kept in mind as we trace Jewish life from the shtetl to the American suburb. The quote is a safeguard that keeps us from putting something holy into relative terms. The study of the Jews' move from the shtetl to the towns and then to America is, in fact, a leap out of Judaism.[15] The man that studied Talmud and Torah all day was more of a Jew than the suburban American dentist. Whether this is good or bad is not at issue. What is at issue is tracing this long road out of what it is to be Jewish; and then completing the journey knowing that deep down the assimilationist is still Jewish. The faith is that he, like the Talmudist, will come through on his Judaism when pushed.

The shtetl of Poland and Russia is where we have to begin our study of the American Jew. The shtetl was a self-contained community, in the pre-political sense, where men communed with each other without the bureaucratic machinery that we now use to sidestep human encounter.[16] This does not mean that there were not many difficulties, but at the same time, you always "knew your lot". Marriage was often arranged while you were still in your mother's womb. The man was the family head, but the family was dad, mom, and kids together rather than today's parents with sons and daughters all over the globe. For all of its rigidity and lack of democracy, the shtetl was a community--something we lack and try to contrive today.[17]

Just as the Amish come to the city today in America, the young Jew in Poland was not going to stay in the shtetl. Young Amish people are being exposed to television and automobiles and they like what the city has to offer. For the eastern European Jew, secular literature started to leak the enlightenment through, the young Jew[8] decided he wanted a piece of that big grand world.[18] Besides the adventure seeker, great numbers of families were forced to the cities for

14

political and economic reasons. It became harder and harder to make a living in the shtetl and in some parts of Russia Jews were forced into certain sections of large cities. In World of Our Fathers Irving Howe concludes that it was impossible for the Jew to live in Russia once the pogroms began:

> The pogroms of 1881 left the Jews stunned and bleeding, it was no longer possible, even for the Russified middle class Jewish intellectuals to hold out much hope for Fabian solutions . . . Neither stability nor peace, well being nor equality, was possible for the Jews of Russia.[19]

But it goes deeper--migration to the city was not totally the result of religious oppression. As I said above the adventure of the enlightenment had found its way to the shtetl. In retrospect, we can see the move to the city as the first step toward America; and, with deeper analysis, the first leap from Judaism. Warsaw and other cities were the enlightenment. Judaism was for the young Jew both rigid and binding. There were too many great and interesting things in the world to be bound by religious roots. Unfortunately for the young Jew his new found freedom was not so easy. The European disease of anti-semitism was not forgotten because he denied his "father's religion". In eastern Europe, a Jew was a Jew was a Jew.

The late nineteenth century brought two movements for Eastern European Jews. There was the continuing Zionistic force which was growing but not yet very strong. It has to be remembered that the young enlightened Jew read Marx and Engels or Emerson and Wordsworth rather than Abraham, Isaac, and Jacob.[20] The word was that America was the place to be rather than the holy land. Like the puritans had said two hundred years earlier, America was the new Jerusalem. The communal movement, Am Olam (Eternal People), began in almost every Polish and Russian city with the goal of communal emigration from eastern Europe to America. Although the great communal land movement of American Jews was never to be, Am Olam was the thrust behind mass Jewish immigration to the United States. Am Olam arranged passage and set up lodging for thousands and thousands of eastern European Jews who wanted to come to America. Howe tells a story about great numbers of people aboard ship carrying the Torah in one hand and Das Kapital in the other. America was the land where the young Jew would be able to express his new-found

15

intellectual freedom.[21] No longer would he be limited inside of his Judaism. Some who study this first movement of eastern European Jewish immigration try to make a case for the Am Olam member as a new type of Jew: no more or no less of a Jew, but just different in kind.[22] Their fathers and their grandfathers had no trouble in analysis; for many, the young emigrants were still their sons and daughters, but they knew America was not Jewish; the more pious lit candles and sat Shiva.[23]

This, though, was only the first wave of emigration. As the century turned, the pogroms and oppression in eastern Europe intensified and great numbers of Jews began to emigrate. No longer was Jewish immigration limited to the young and "enlightened". Many people left for Israel and many more worked hard to reach America. Family helped bring over family, and friends brought over friends. By 1905 the lower east side of New York was the Jewish immigrant.[24] It is in this section of New York that the Jewish American experience begins. It becomes an experience rather than the Jewish condition because in America the direction is upward and outward rather than being part of something; in this case the Jewish condition. But enlightened as the young Jew claimed to be, the contradiction between what it was to be Jewish and what it was to be American was not an easy contradiction for him to bridge. When religious custom came up against his new found freedom his choices were not easy. Guilt was not avoided when he broke the Sabbath but nevertheless the ritual was often not observed.[25] It appears that even the most ardent non-believers had trouble with their non-belief. Socialist and anarchist groups held Yom Kippur Balls in protest of the holiest holiday of the year. In analyzing I have to wonder why they would protest something that no longer had any meaning.[26]

What the Jew met in New York was not just great intellectual freedom. Like the Irishman before him, the Jewish immigrant lived poorly when he came to the lower east side.[27] The tenements were living hell and the sweatshop jobs might have been worse than that. In his book, How the Other Half Lives, Jacob Riis describes tenement life. Over-crowded buildings, health problems, and uncaring landlords are discussed in Riis' work.[28] In the sweatshop you worked long hours for meager pay in conditions that were at best inhuman. Irving Howe quotes from an industrialism report:

16

The contractor . . .would go to the
manufacturer. Finding that there was but
little work to be had he would offer to take
the coats cheaper than the price theretofore
paid. When he came home, he would tell his
men that there was not much work and he was
obliged to take it cheaper, and since he did
not want to reduce their wages and pay them
less per day all they would have to do would
be to make another coat in the task. That
is, if they were accustomed to make 9 coats
in the task, they would be required to make
ten, and then 11, and so on. The wages were
always reduced on the theory that they were
not reduced at all but the amount of labor
increased. In this way intense speed was
developed. The men who had been accustomed
to making 9 coats in a task would make ten,
and so on, up to 15, 18, and even 20, as is
the customary task at the present time
(1901). The hours began to be increased, in
order to make the task in a day.[29]

One question that we can never totally answer is
to what extent was it their great sense of Jewishness
that pulled them through these rough times. Was it
family and community--two major Jewish forces--rather
than the great American dream that was overriding?
Unfortunately or fortunately, the answer is left a
mystery.

What we do know is that as the Jew became more
American the less was he Jewish. This can be seen
through:

1.   The place   of worship; it even changed
names--no longer the Shul or Temple--but now the
synagogue.

2.   The family.

3.   The business world.

When the eastern European Jews settled in New York
there was no such thing as Orthodox, Conservative, or
Reform. The Shul was the place of worship and although
not as everpresent as in Europe it was the center of
the community's religious affairs. The men still went
everyday and religious piety was law. It was still the
center of Jewish community life.[30] In the late 1880's

17

other things--American things--were beginning to take
up more time for the American Jew. The high holidays
and a few token appearances in Shul were the rule
rather than the exception. There were pangs of guilt
but this was America. The small number that remained
pious knew the beginning of the end.[31] In the shtetl
there had always been a chief rabbi who was the
community's spiritual leader.[32] He settled disputes
for there was no dichotomy between secular and
religious. The stories in Isaac Bashevis Singer's In
My Father's Court are about people coming to his
father, who was the chief rabbi, to settle both
religious and secular affairs. A tremendous wealth of
what it was to be Jewish comes from this book. The
reality and the vitality of the people is evident as
emotions run the gamut of love, hate, jealousy, and
trust. One thing you do not have to search for is
personal involvement. The rabbi was an essential and a
vital part of the community.[33]

        As a last try for piety a group that called
themselves The Association of American Hebrew Orthodox
Congregations brought over Rabbi Jacob Joseph from
Vilna. Rabbi Jacob Joseph was to be chief rabbi in
America just as the shtetl had its chief rabbi. The
American Jew, though, had new problems that were
economic, social, and domestic; he did not have time
for religious "hassles". On the more gentle side, even
if he suffered internally from impiety, how could he
touch or be touched by Rabbi Jacob Joseph. In the
shtetl he and the rabbi were kindred spirits; in New
York the chief rabbi could be no more than an
abstraction. There was an economic side also. The
kosher meat packing houses were not about to put up
with his stringent piety. There was money to be made
and they were not going to allow religious rigidity to
cut into the profits.[34] The person that probably
suffered greatest from this last gasp was Rabbi Jacob
Joseph. He, like many others, died in a land he
neither wanted to be in nor was able to understand.

        There are still Orthodox congregations in American
cities. The number of pious Jews--Yeshiva goers[35] and
old world Orthodox--is very small. For the most part,
even the Orthodox congregation is full only on the high
holidays. Seemingly a contradiction to stay Orthodox
and be unobservant, the logic might be that if I am
going to hold on, it may as well be to the best. In a
sense this, too, is a last grasping at spirituality.

The contradiction was too much for some of the young who wanted to hold religion but be American at the same time. Some chose the Young Israel movement--an English rather than Hebrew Orthodoxy. The Young Israel movement did not think that American dress and social habits were irreverent.[56] About the time of World War I, Conservative Judaism began to attract membership in America. Devoid of the cruder European customs, Conservative Judaism mirrored America.[57] The Bible was living, thus Judaism had to suit the times. More money was being made and the new synagogues reflected the move up. In the beginning, Conservative Judaism was like the man with one foot in and one foot out. He wanted tradition but he also had to keep pace with the times. Theoretically, the task seems noble; unfortunately the two sides are antithetical. Half seems better than nothing but for some adults and many children it was a bifurcated world. You are taught one thing at Hebrew school, but daily activities more often than not contradict the religious teachings.

This brings us to the reform movement. Although strongly German, Reform Judaism still touches the Jew from Eastern Europe. Reform Judaism had its beginnings in late nineteenth century Germany. The progressive era in America saw the spreading out of the Reform synagogue. Reform Judaism is characteristic of the time of its growth for the progressive era meant, intellectually, not believing in anything too strongly.[58] It is logical to see Reform Judaism naturally following Orthodox then Conservative. The Conservatives knew German Reform Judaism, though, and the traditional Conservative was trying to avoid Reform Judaism. He saw it as the final negation. The logic is right, though, in noting that Reform Judaism had to come to the Jewish immigrant from eastern Europe. The contradiction the Reform Jew tried to escape was now sanctioned but was no less of a contradiction. How else could the American Jew disregard the Sabbath, eat "Traif,"[59] and still be no less of a Jew. Eric Goldman describes a meeting of Reform rabbis in Rendevous With Destiny.

> Nineteen rabbis from various parts of the country assembled in Pittsburgh to draw up the first comprehensive statement of 'Reform Judaism'. By Reform these men primarily meant changes in customs and dogma, such as the abolition of the ancient prohibition on the eating of pork, the use of English prayers in synagogue services, and denial of

19

the doctrine that Jews should restore a
Jewish state in Palestine.[40]

It was felt that these changes were essential to keep
the Jewish religion in touch with the modern world.
This assumption cannot be brought to issue. The issue
is that Reform Judaism created something new and
different. Whatever that something new and different
is, it is not the Judaism of the shul. To make it
relative and put it on a continuum with the shul is to
lessen something meaningful and substantial. The move
from the city to the suburbs, growing wealth, and
becoming more American, all go together. In the above
we find the essence of the Reform synagogue. Religion
could now occupy its proper place in the American
genre. Still, Reform Jews argue that it is just
another type of Judaism, no more or no less. It is
this type of statement that brings to mind this year's
Passover Seder.[41] An important part of the Seder is
when the youngest son asks his father to explain
Passover; it is called the four questions. When my dad
asked his father, he said that he did not think about
it; he was expected to know them and he knew them. He
did not think about it but just did it. When it became
my turn I worried that I would forget. I memorized
them and practiced so I would not forget. Maybe the
four quesitons were not internalized but they were
still present. Today, like my dad, the kids do not
think about it; the difference is they do not know
them. This cannot be made relative. The old world
orthodox is more Jewish than the American reform; to
make it an issue and open it for debate trivializes
something of meaning.

The family, like the synagogue, helps trace
American Judaism. The strength of the shtetl family
was never to be repeated yet the early Jewish family in
America was still powerful. The father could no longer
spend his day at the study house and this in itself
made him less of a Jew; and, for himself, less of a
man.[42] The woman in America continued with much of the
same activities as in the shtetl. Along with running
the house and the kids she bought and sold wares and
mastered or was mastered in the market place.[43] In a
strange land the family was the one source of
stability. Within those walls the language was still
Yiddish, the food was still familiar, and the family
was still a family, almost even in the old world sense
of family. It is again from Singer's work that we meet
the old world Jewish family. The tribal concept of
family members each having binding responsibilities was

very much part of the shtetl family. If there was a small business everyone was involved in the day's work. There was a definite distinction between parent and child but it was a cohesive unit of people working not only for each other but with each other. There was no binding concept of family through law or edict, the family just bound. People did not sit down and define their family roles but each knew his place within the family. Of course it was not problem free and there were times when the house closed in around you. Human misery was present as was human joy and both were shared as a family. Family members were part of each other and took care of each other. And it was in the family that the individual belonged.

This, though, is the new, not the old, and family for the new becomes a paradox. Although scared of the new land, the old world parent wanted his kids to make it in America. He knew his own sweat and toil and wanted a better world for his children. The better world meant being American. The turn of the century meant public schools for Jewish children. With all the good that goes with this event it goes against the very grain of the Jewish family. [44] No longer can life revolve around a "kitchen culture". No longer can old world religious customs and "superstitions" have substance for those who are educated. [45] The paradox is that the education dad and mom wanted for son and daughter was the cause of family estrangement. Dad and mom were proud of son and daughter, but their worlds were divided. Son and daughter were proud and grateful but at the same time were embarrassed by old world ways. The stories of six year old kids telling their folks to "stop speaking Yiddish, English is spoken in America," are rule rather than exception. The hard part to get is that although mom and dad and son and daughter fought over old and new, it was mom and dad that wanted the kids to make it as Americans. And mom and dad wanted the kids to make it knowing full well that making it meant being less Jewish and being less Jewish meant the breakup of the family. Embarrassed by the ways of their folks meant spending less time at home and more time being American. Less time at home diminished the importance of the family and other things; business, intellectual and social; took its place. [46] The sad part, but the reality, of the situation, is that there is a price to pay for moving onward and upward; the estrangement of family is one of the costs of being American. Now <u>folks</u> become <u>parents</u> because father and son no longer know each other. This is exemplified in the writings of Jewish novelists

Philip Roth and Saul Bellow. You walk away from their
work knowing you have met estranged man. Not only do
father and son not know each other but families of four
live in Cleveland and Los Angeles and Oregon. We are
spread out all over North America. This obviously is
not exceptional to the American Jew. But for the Jew
it is the breakdown of what it is to be Jewish. The
family, once an essential part of Judaism, is no longer
the family. Again, some say it is just a new type, one
of many kinds; but that perverts the meaning of family.
(A shtetl family of ten would turn over) Like the shul
the decline of the family is part of the price we pay
to be American.

      The work of the Jew in America led him away from
the lower east side. Just as high school and then
college diplomas meant moving out, so did changing
occupations. The 1890's and the first twenty years of
the twentieth century saw very few jobs open to the
immigrant Jew. Sweatshop work meant many hours but
little pay. The problem was there was little choice in
what a man could do to make a living. Some avoided the
sweatshop and peddled goods but the money was not any
better and, if possible, the security was less. This,
though, was the land of a dream and the eastern
European immigrant was determined to live it.[47] Bud
Schulberg's What Makes Sammy Run is literary example of
the drive, amongst other things, that possessed many of
the young. In Schulberg's book Sammy is willing to do
anything to get ahead in the business world. Raises,
promotions, and wealth stand over and above everything
else. Everyone of course was not Sammy but for some it
was a way of life. With the help of already rich
German Jews a number of roads to the American bourgeois
middle class were opened. Salesmen, teachers,
secretaries, and lawyers, were occupations opening up
for young Jews as the first world war approached. The
great numbers still worked in factories (garment and
cigar) but they did not believe in like father, like
son. Their sweat and blood was so their kids could
escape. After all that was one of the reasons they
came to this country. Besides the occupations listed
above, small businesses were opened: drugstores,
butcher shops, clothes shops, etc. This led to certain
so-called Jewish industries including garment, scrap
iron, and real estate.[48] Each new conquest meant
entering the world to a greater degree and moving away
from the lower east side was not uncommon. Closing the
store on the Sabbath meant losing business and more and
more stores opened their doors. A small thing for the
outside observer but another break from what it is to

22

be Jewish. In a book called The Sabbath, Jewish
theologian Abraham Heschel views the American Jews
unobservance of the sabbath as one of the most tragic
breakdowns of the religion. For Heschel, the Sabbath
as a different day than the other days of the week was
a binding and spiritual force.[49] But as Americans it
is impossible to deal with this issue as good or bad.
What we can do is look at the vast occupations of Jews
in America today and see that it takes them all over
the continent. Just as other Americans, the Jew lives
everywhere from Seattle to Miami (more so Miami). The
butcher's son is scientist for Boeing--he has cashed in
on the American dream, and to do it he has had to be
less Jewish. Mom and dad in New York City and son in
Seattle dilutes the Jewish tradition.

One industry that might over-generalize but still
serves as a good example is the movie industry. Going
off to make it in tinsel town is the prototype of
absolute rejection of everything Jewish. The Moguls by
Norman Zierold describes the lives of those that
created Nathaniel West's Day of the Locust. The
absolute denial of Judaism is seen in the actions of
the movie magnate Selznicks. Zierol's book describes
the moguls as men who would stop at no ends in order to
get what they were after. Family breakups, big time
gambling, drinking and carousing were rule rather than
exception according to Zierold.[50] They opted for a new
life and what they did was part of what it was to
choose the gold rush. One sad but amusing incident
involved Jesse Lasky of Paramount:

> When Jesse Lasky of Paramount was taken
> to the hospital with a heart attack he
> unhesitatingly replied 'American' to a
> routine question about race. 'Now, now, Mr.
> Lasky,' said the sweet little Hebrew lady
> behind the desk. 'We're Jewish aren't we.'
> 'Jewish? Oh yes, yes Jewish,' said the
> surprised Lasky.[51]

Lasky's first answer might have been the right one.
Going to a reform synagogue once a year, having family
spread all over the land, and climbing the job scale or
seeking the gold rush is what it is to be an
"American". Lasky, like us, is American; day in and
day out, our choices are antithetical to what it is to
be Jewish. We left that to be American and you cannot
have both.

The Rise of David Levinsky, a novel written by

Abraham Cahan, long time editor of The Jewish Daily Forward,[52] traces the above journey. Cahan exhibits his longing for something gone knowing it is gone forever. David Levinsky works in the sweatshop, he becomes a peddler, he studies and he teaches. He decides to be a doctor and ends up a garment magnate. Though never ready to give back American success, Levinsky longs for much of the old: a family as he knew it in the old world, a shul where the people knew each other. He knew this could not be had by just going to the synagogue on the high holidays. Nevertheless, his longing did not stop him from skipping even Yom Kippur if business called. Cahan's longing through Levinsky was admittance of the end of one chapter and the beginning of another. He knew there was no going back. The Forward doubled as the last gasp of the old and the bridge to the new. It was a bridge to the new because it explained to the reader the proper way to become American. Articles were about American things: hamburgers, hot dogs, the Ford, the pros and cons of baseball (The Forward was a pro). It was a guide for the lower east side Jew in Americanization--all the time doing it in Yiddish; that is why it was a last gasp. It tried to better the lot and bettering the lot meant becoming American.

The Jewish immigrant was not peculiar in wanting to be American. Being American meant getting a cut of the action and that is why the immigrants first came to Ellis Island. What was peculiar to America was that everyone was an outsider and it meant there was room for everyone to move.[53] Each group knew the American dream and each group wanted in. Since everyone was a stranger, the middle class was accessible to all--or almost all: we still have to deal with American racism.[54] But for the immigrant the melting pot was not an abstraction; or was it?

This issue is still being argued today. Samuel Lubell, in his book The Future of American Politics, makes a case for America as the melting pot. Lubell writes of the melting pot from an economic point of view. As the immigrant's economic base broadened he became more American and less European:[55]

> With more jobs than workers, wages soar.
> Occupations barred to minorities are flung
> open. Jobs become available for all members
> of a family capable of work. This is
> particularly important for poor people with
> their larger families. The family overhead

24

does not change much with three or four breadwinners instead of one, but income spurts spectacularly. The more thrifty families save their surplus earnings. On the strength of those savings they keep their children in school longer, even pushing them on through college. They also flee their ethnic ghettos for nicer residential areas.[56]

Lubell continues with what happens as the immigrant forms an economic foundation:

There has been much pooh-poohing of social climbing without appreciation of the fact that it is a vital part of the Americanization process. The move to a 'nicer' neighborhood would often be celebrated by a shortening or anglicizing of names. Items of alien garb would be dropped; foreign accents would lighten. There would be more American food in the grocery stores, less orthodoxy in worship, more intermarriage with other ethnics elements and an ironical index of Americanization--more divorce.[57]

For Lubell social changes followed economic changes and they were both part of becoming American. Over and over again the birthright is sold and the above is part of what the melting pot means.

In Beyond the Melting Pot, Daniel Moynihan and Nathan Glazer disclaim the melting pot. Although they study New York City, their book is a microcosm of the country as a whole. They claim that the term "melting pot" is a misnomer and that ethnic interests are strong and divisive.[58] For Moynihan and Glazer there is no such thing as an American, but rather ethnic identities that give us a pluralistic ethnicity:

Socially it lost its identifying power and when you asked a man what he was (in the United States), 'American' was not the answer you were looking for. In the United States it became a slogan, a political gesture, sometimes an evasion, but not a matter of course social description of a person. Just as in certain languages a word cannot stand alone but needs some particle to indicate its function, so in the United States the word 'American' does not stand by itself.[59]

25

They continue by discussing ethnicity in America as
something new and different than in the old world but
nevertheless ethnic in culture. Certain things are
distinctly Jewish while other things are peculiar to
Italians. The Jews still abhor and are terrified of
intermarriage with the gentiles. In fact, synagogues
have increased their membership. Italian suburbanites
are sending their children back to the Catholic school.
Moynihan and Glazer conclude that these distinct
difference between Jew and Italian are the types of
things that make the melting pot an illusion.[60] Others
like Peter Schrag and Michael Novak call the "melting
pot" a myth. They argue that Americanization was the
death of the immigrant rather than the melting together
of the different ethnics to make "America".[61] But
Schrag and Novak, like Moynihan and Glazer, believe
that ethnic differences are real and that those
differences will always stand.

Oscar Handlin does not deny the differences but
still makes a case for America as the melting pot. The
Uprooted studies two centuries of America taking in
immigrant groups. Handlin discusses the American dream
and claims that most of the differences between groups
are now form rather than substance.[62] He makes you
realize that bagels and lox do not make you Jewish just
as blacklava does not make you Greek:

> Despite the sentimental value set on
> ethnicity, fewer differences among the groups
> seemed worth preserving. Distinctive
> religious and ethnic characteristics faded
> and trained technically professional
> bureaucrats took charge so that one
> institution was very similar to another. The
> more alike Beth Israel and St. Elizabeth
> became the less reason there was to preserve
> their separateness, the more reason to mingle
> their services under the auspices of the
> government that could pay for all.[63]

Americans attend the public school, move to the
suburbs, and become more and more alike as time goes
on. As Handlin points out even the things that are
peculiar to one group are losing their distinctiveness.
One case that might be watched is the Catholic schools.
Now that they are getting federal funding, will they
become less "Catholic" and more "public". With federal
funds come government restrictions and whether or not
these restrictions make the schools more secular is a
real question. For America, it might be that

26

everything is public. We neither can nor want to
sustain tradition when everything around us is contrary
to it. Bernard Mehl explains it well in The Review of
Education.

> I grew up with Jewish children whose
> grandfathers spoke Yiddish, refused to drive
> on the Sabbath, were solidly Orthodox and
> lost in the comfortable atmosphere of Long
> Island. The grandfathers believed they were
> chosen by God to carry on the Law in the face
> of the 'goyim' who only upheld a belief in
> the greatest good for the greatest number.
> The fathers went, instead, to the
> Conservative synagogue and were worried about
> the Jewish image. Einstein, yes--Louis
> Lepke, the gangster, no. The fathers played
> down the chosen aspect of being Jewish and
> sent their children to college. The children
> fought in World War II and joined the
> Reformed Temple. Their children now deny
> being chosen because it's a sign of
> exclusiveness and they say that no one is
> better than anyone else. My friend's
> children are now Jewish moral relativists who
> would give equal time to Moses and to the
> overseer.[64]

Professor Mehl's experiences run parallel to the
literature that is being written concerning the modern
day American Jew. Judaism has become less important
with each generation. My generation (I am 35) says "my
parents were Jewish but I'm not any religion". But
again, it has to be remembered that this is not
peculiar to the American Jew. It might be that it is
part of what it means to be American. Professor Mehl
continues discussing fragmentation and the public
school:

> The American ethos is by its nature
> fragmentary in its evolution. Having no
> history in tradition, aristocratic or ethnic,
> it is doomed to fly apart--making the body
> politic an easy prey for totalitarianism.
> Hannah Arendt supports the thesis that
> totalitarianism comes when romantic
> rootlessness takes over historical tradition.
> the American experience needs to counter the
> nonhistorical aspect of its development with
> a sense of Providence. In Mannheim's terms,
> since America rejects a faith in the

absolute, it needs a sense of utopian
thinking to curb the intercine nature of
ideology. The American public school is the
institution which makes certain that utopian
thinking is people-centered and not a product
of an elite. Elites dominate whether they be
businessmen who want willing consumers, or
labor leaders who want dues-paying members,
or homosexuals who want gay liberation. Yet
is spite of separate dominations endemic in
America, the special aspect of the American
public school maintains continuity with a
utopian past which declares that all men are
created equal.[65]

It is the relationship of this rootlessness and
equality, in America, that has been reviewed in this
chapter. The melting pot, equality, and progress as
well as alienation and fragmentation have been examined
through the lives of the Jewish immigrant. With the
rootlessness and the equality cited in the quote above
in mind, we can turn to the public school and the
immigrant. The schooling of the immigrant should help
us to understand the tension between the elitism and
the equality that is part of America's history.

28

Footnotes

[1]C. Wright Mills, <u>Power, Politics, and People</u> (New York: Ballantine Books, 1963), p. 211.

[2]C. Wright, Mills, <u>White Collar</u>, p. xvi.

[3]<u>Ibid</u>.

[4]<u>Ibid</u>., p. xiii.

[5]George M. Stephenson, <u>A History of American Immigration</u> (New York: Ginn & Co., 1926), p. 61.

[6]<u>Ibid</u>., p. 64.

[7]<u>Ibid</u>., p. 73.

[8]<u>Ibid</u>., p. 87.

[9]Carlos Levi, <u>Christ Stopped at Eboli</u> (New York: Farrar, Straus and Giroux, 1963), p. 123.

[10]<u>Ibid</u>., p. 131.

[11]H. Arnold Barton, <u>Letters From the Promised Land</u> (Minneapolis: University of Minnesota Press, 1975), p. 286.

[12]Frederick Haskin, <u>The Immigrant</u> (New York: Fleming H. Revell Co., 1913), p. 45.

[13]Oscar Handlin, <u>The Uprooted</u> (Boston and Toronto: Little, Brown and Company, 1951). pp. 34-35.

[14]Fydor Dostoyevsky, <u>The Brothers Karamozov</u> (New York: 1957), p. 217.

[15]Paul Rosenblatt and Gene Koppel, <u>A Certain Bridge: Isaac B. Singer on Literature and Life</u> (Tucson: University of Arizona Press, 1971).

[16]Isaac Bashevis Singer, <u>In My Father's Court</u> (New York: Straus and Giroux, 1962), Introduction and Chapter I.

[17]<u>Ibid</u>., pp. vii-viii.

[18]Irving Howe, <u>World of Our Fathers</u> (New York: Harcourt Brace Jovanovich, 1976), pp. 29-34.

[19]Ibid., p. 7.

[20]Irving Malin, Critical Views of Isaac Bashevis Singer (New York: New York University Press, 1969), p. 15.

[21]Irving Howe, World of Our Fathers (New York: Harcourt Brace Jovanovich, 1976), pp. 29-34.

[22]Ibid.

[23]Shiva is a one week observance remembering someone who has just died.

[24]Jacob Riis, How the Other Half Lives (New York: Hill & Wang, 1957), pp. 76-86.

[25]Howe, World of Our Fathers, p. 191.

[26]Ibid., p. 106.

[27]Ibid., pp. 148-158.

[28]Jacob Riis, How the Other Half Lives (New York: Hill & Wang, 1957), p. 76.

[29]Irving Howe, World of Our Fathers (New York: Harcourt Brace Jovanovich, 1976), p. 156.

[30]Ibid., p. 190.

[31]Ibid., pp. 194-195.

[32]Isaac Bashevis Singer, In My Father's Court (New York: Straus, and Giroux, 1962), pp. vii-viii.

[33]Ibid.

[34]Irving Howe, World of Our Fathers (New York: Harcourt Brace Jovanovich, 1976), p. 194.

[35]The Yeshiva is a religious school that stresses the daily study of Torah and Talmud. If there is anything secular it is only because of state credential laws and even then it is very minor.

[36]Howe, World of Our Fathers, pp. 197-198.

[37]Ibid., p. 198.

[38]Goldman, Rendezvous With Destiny, p. 173.

[39]Traif is unkosher food.

[40]Goldman, Rendezvous With Destiny, p. 173.

[41]The seder commemorates the Jews being freed from slavery in Egypt.

[42]Abraham Cahan, The Rise of David Levinsky (New York: Harper & Brothers, 1917), pp. 95-97.

[43]Howe, World of Our Fathers, p. 260.

[44]Ibid., pp. 256-287.

[45]Ibid., pp. 261-262.

[46]Ibid., pp. 256-287.

[47]Cahan, The Rise of David Levinsky, pp. 480-485.

[48]Howe, World of Our Fathers, pp. 165-168.

[49]Abraham Heschel, The Sabbath (New York: Farrar, Strauss, and Young, 1951), Chapter 1.

[50]Norman Zierold, The Moguls (New York: Coward-McCann, 1969), pp. 13-83.

[51]Ibid., p. 10.

[52]The Jewish Daily Forward is a national daily Yiddish newspaper.

[53]Michael Harrington, The Other America (New York: Macmillan Co., 1964), p. 7.

[54]Ibid., pp. 7-8 and 61-82.

[55]Samuel Lubell, The Future of American Politics (New York: Harper and Brothers, 1951), pp. 68-69.

[56]Ibid., p. 69.

[57]Ibid., p. 62.

[58]Nathan Glazer and Daniel Patrick Moynihan, Beyond the Melting Pot (Cambridge, Massachusetts: The MIT Press, 1970), p. 15.

[59]Ibid.

[60] Ibid.

[61] Mark Krug, The Melting of the Ethnics, pp. 5, 100.

[62] Handlin, The Uprooted, pp. 280-284.

[63] Ibid., p. 284.

[64] Mehl, "Who's Liberated," The Review of Education, August, 1976, p. 395.

[65] Ibid., p. 396.

CHAPTER 3

THE SCHOOLING OF THE IMMIGRANT--AN OVERVIEW

When Horace Mann began lobbying for public education there were many people that had to be pleased. The masses were feared by the monied class and it was to the monied class that he spoke of the schools as agents of social control. How else could the masses vote and their heart be in the right place? At the same time, to the masses the schooling of their children was frivolous at a time when each hand was needed for work. It was to this group that Mann spoke of equality, opportunity, and social mobility.[1] The schools were to be their ticket to the American dream. The truth might be that Mann was not lying to either group. This tension in American education between elitism and equality might be the strange paradox that is essential to the American school? The tension continued through the nineteenth century and, if anything, intensified with the great wave of immigration from southern and eastern Europe at the turn of the twentieth century. Great numbers of immigrants descended on the American cities. There weren't enough jobs and the newcomers threatened the already overcrowded job market. The "answer" was the public school and Perkinson tells us that the tension between control and equality still existed:[2]

> The city child, especially the child of the newcomers, had generated both compassion and fear. He was unkempt, uncared for, and untutored. He was in need of help. But he also was a threat, a threat to the workingman, a threat to social customs, mores, and institutions, a threat to the future of American democracy. Partly from fear and partly from compassion, thirty one states enacted some form of compulsory education law by 1900.[3]

The public school has been called the religion of America many, many times. The tremendous faith that developed is one of the reasons why education can be called on as the "answer" over and over again. In The American Faith In the Schools As An Agency of Progress: Promise and Fulfillment, Jeffrey Herold documents this faith from the time of the Puritans to Lyndon Baines Johnson's "Great Society". The different stages in American history looked to education with different desires but the same faith appears to be everpresent:[4]

Interpreting the American school as a church not only helps us understand more clearly the intensity of American faith in the schools, but it helps us understand the rhetoric and behavior of American educators. Just as the priests and ministers of the Christian Church went out into the world filled with missionary zeal, so too have American educators manifested a sense of mission, a zeal to win converts to education, to improve the behavior of individuals, and ultimately to save men and society. American educators have behaved somewhat as priests of progress.[5]

The question that still has to be asked about the immigrant and the school is--did the school control the immigrant and make him submissive? Or was the school an equalizer that sustained the American dream and made America the melting pot of equality?

In his dissertation, The Pathological Model and the Schools: A Critical Inquiry, Richard Nelson steals a phrase from Eric Goldman and calls the early progressives "reform Darwinists".[6] Reform Darwinism was a reaction to the social Darwinism of Herbert Spencer and William Graham Sumner. Spencer and Sumner used Darwin's theory of evolution to profess a theory of social and economic determinism.[7] In Social Darwinism in American Thought, Richard Hofstadter reviews and analyzes Sumner's work:

Social advance depends primarily upon hereditary wealth; for wealth offers a premium to effort, and hereditary wealth assures the enterprising and industrious man that he may preserve in his children the virtues which have enabled him to enrich the community.[8]

Equality and the rights of man are negated by both Spencer and Sumner. In fact they were thought of as being silly because the natural process could not be overcome.[9] Hofstadter ends his chapter on Sumner with a telling analogy: "Like some latter-day Calvin, he came to preach the predestination of the social order and the Salvation of the economically elect through the survival of the fittest."[10]

As I said above the reaction to social Darwinism is now called reform Darwinism. The criticism leveled by liberal sociologist Frank Lester Ward (a reform Darwinist) in his book, Dynamic Sociology, was that social Darwinism took a scientific theory and used it to sustain elitist ideology.[11] Hofstadter discusses Ward's thesis on social Darwinism as an elitist theory:

> His advocacy of state management was prompted by a lower class bias. He seems to have considered himself a lobbyist for the people in academic forums. His opposition to the biological argument for individualism stemmed from his democratic faith; his rejection of Sumner and Spencer was partly motivated by his sense of their aristocratic preferences.[12]

For Ward there were problems but all we had to do was to control the environment in order to solve them. The answer to America's ills was environmental expertise. Hofstadter tells us that Ward wanted the title of Dynamic Sociology to be The Great Panacea. Ward truly believed that education and social engineering could control the environment and cure society's ills:[13]

> A sociocratic world would distribute its favors according to merit, as individualists demand, but by equalizing opportunity for all it would eliminate advantages now possessed by those with undeserved power, accidental position or wealth, or anti-social cunning.[14]

Ward felt that through the expert we would educate and do what was right for mankind. Nelson discusses the sociology of two of these experts, Charles Cooly and E. A. Ross, who feared the immigrants and opted for social control in the name of democaracy. And even Jane Addams, who was warm and gentle, thought of the immigrants as children who had to be shown the way. The pathological mind-set assumes that some are well and others sick.[15] The sick must be cured.

For the reform Darwinists the sick were the immigrants. A New York City social worker, Robert Hunter, tells about losing touch with his own land. "I was an utter stranger in my own city."[16] He goes on with tremendous fear, feeling deeply threatened:

> The direct descendents of the people who fought for and found the Republic and who

35

gave us a rich heritage of democratic institutions are being displaced by the slavic Balkan and Mediterranean peoples.[17]

Hunter voiced concern over the growing birth rate and he stressed the need for some type of intelligent social control.

Through an understanding of people like Hunter as well as the writings of W. E. B. Dubois, Nelson argues that reform Darwinism just like social Darwinism was an ideological position.[18] An ideological position in the Mannheim sense of the term where there was both a psychological and social model.[19] Nelson writes about Dubois' belief in expertise as well as his reversal:

> Dubois was one of the first Americans to realize the ideological basis of the apparently objective studies of science. Rather than being an escape from relativity through universal objective truth it had revealed itself as an ideological tool. With Dostoevski he realized that the love of humanity in general covered an inability to love man in the particular.[20]

The reform Darwinist position could not help but be ideological. The basic assumption of expertise that cures ills preassumes a world of "we" and "them". Social workers like Jane Addams and reform political candidates were puzzled and appalled when immigrant[21] groups again and again elected crooked ward bosses. After all the reform candidates were only working with the best interests of the immigrant groups in mind. But the truth that Miss Addams came to understand was that the ward bosses were of and with the people while the social workers were outside of and above the people.[22] The immigrant often knew that the social worker wasn't with him but rather was working on him. Bernard Mehl referred to the cadre of experts as "psychic cops".[23] It might be that the immigrant was well aware of their presence before the phrase was coined.

The same kind of pathological ideology discussed above, the same fear, and sometimes the same bitterness, did not elude education. In Changing Conceptions of Education, published in 1909, Ellwood P. Cubberley makes a great distinction between the new immigrants, those from eastern and southern Europe, and

the Irish and Germans who preceded them.[24]   For
Cubberley, knowing that the "Anglo-Saxon" virtues were
the right ones was all-important. He said that the old
immigrants were well aware of these Anglo-Saxon tenets
but that the new immigrants were a different breed, a
threat.[25]

> These southern and eastern Europeans are
> of a very different type from the north
> Europeans who preceded them.   Illiterate,
> docile, lacking in self-reliance and
> initiative, and not possessing the
> Anglo-Teutonic conceptions of law, order, and
> government, their coming has served to dilute
> tremendously our national stock, and to
> corrupt our civic life. The great bulk of
> these people have settled in the cities of
> the North Atlantic and North Central states,
> and the problems of proper housing and
> living, moral and sanitary conditions, honest
> and decent government, and proper education
> have everywhere been made more difficult by
> their presence . . . Our task is to break up
> these groups or settlements, to assimilate
> and amalgamate these people as a part of our
> American race, and to implant in their
> children, so far as can be done, the
> Anglo-Saxon concept of righteousness, law and
> order, and popular government, and to awaken
> in them a reverence for our democratic
> institutions and for those things in our
> nation which we as a people hold to be of
> abiding worth.[26]

Cubberley continues by discussing the bad effects the
new immigrants had already had on what he calls
"Anglo-Saxon righteousness". It's almost: if we don't
get them, they will get us. And for Cubberley, the way
to get to the immigrant with our Anglo-Saxon tenets is
through the public school.[27] In spite of the above, he
lets equality slip in, and mentions the schools as a
stepladder, even for the new immigrant. His belief is
that education can cure the immigrant and make him
American.[28]

The same attitude, although a little more gentle,
is found in early twentieth century Boston school
superintendent, Frank V. Thompson's Schooling of the
Immigrant.   Thompson is a cultist of efficiency who
believed the schools should have a better plan to deal
with the immigrants. He too looks at the immigrants as

a disease that has to be cured. He compares the immigrant child to the mentally deficient child. "The same philosophy which justifies variation of treatment for the mentally atypical would justify variation in the case of the socially atypical child."[29]

Again the immigrant is that "other" that has to be worked on by the people that are in the know. Sartre called it the "science of mediocrity" in his book Anti-Semite and Jew. The mediocre man sustains life by making something lower than himself.[30]

> By treating the Jew as an inferior and pernicious being, I affirm at the same time that I belong to the elite. This elite, in contrast to those of modern times which are based on merit or labor, closely resembles an aristocracy of birth. There is nothing I have to do to merit my superiority, and neither can I lose it. It is given once and for all. It is a thing.[31]

Sartre continues by analyzing the great dependency of the anti-semite. There has to be an "other" and for mediocre man who the other is is unimportant. "The Jew only serves him as a pretext; elsewhere his counterpart will make use of the Negro or the man of yellow skin."[32] In this case the "other" is the "new immigrant," but sustaining the position is most difficult. After all, you scratch an American deep enough and you find an immigrant. In America our equivalent to European anti-semitism is our pathological view of what it is is to be Black. Sociologist Gunnar Myrdal calls it The American Dilemma and says that racism is endemic to America. W. J. Cash in his book The Mind of the South tells us how difficult it is to sustain the lie. The lengths that were gone to in order for the southerner to convince himself that "white is right" is in itself evident that it is a lie.[33] Cash calls it the "southern ego" and he says that it needed continual reaffirmation of its superiority. This sustenance came through creation of biological, theological, and political theory. Cash tells us that the ante had to be continually raised because the inauthenticity was all too clear.[34] But now back to the schooling of the immigrant.

Thompson did not fear the immigrant as much as Cubberley. He felt that the right kind of teaching would make the immigrant American. He abhorred physical force but felt that persuasion through

38

education would surely Americanize the immigrant.[35] Thompson knew it was already happening in the schools unconsciously but what was needed was an all-out plan for Americanization. He submitted a plan for national and state boards to control the education of immigrants. Only if they were taught to be Americans in the schools would they become one of us.[36]

Whether the reality of the public schools is synonymous with the ideology of social control is still in question. The answer is probably both yes and no. To think that Cubberley or Ross or Cooly were the only ones that thought as they did is at best silly. Most likely, there were teachers that agreed and many others that didn't. There are a group of educators that are writing today who believe that social control was the reality in the schooling of the immigrant. This group, labeled "the revisionists," takes on what they call "the myth of the public school and the American dream." Included are Colin Greer, Michael Katz, Clarence J. Karier, and Paul Violas. Their criticism in most general terms is that the public schools have always been a tool of the social elite to keep the masses in their place. Educators like Cubberley and teachers and administrators are pawns who police this social control. In her book, The Revisionists Revised, Professor Diane Ravitch states the themes of the revisionists:

> Several themes deriving from this perspective appear in the radical histories. First, the school was used by the rich and the middle class as an instrument to manipulate and control the poor and the working class. Second, efforts to extend schooling to greater numbers and to reform the schools were primarily middle-class morality campaigns intended to enhance the coercive power of the school. Third, an essential purpose of the school was to stamp our cultural diversity and to advance homogeneity. Fourth, the idea that upward social mobility might be achieved by children of the poor through schooling, was a fable. Fifth, bureaucracy was deliberately selected as the most appropriate structure for perpetuating social stratification by race, sex, and social class. Sixth, a primary function of schooling was to serve the needs of capitalism by instilling appropriate work habits in future workers. Seventh, those

liberals and progressives who tried to make the schools better were serving the interest of the status quo. Lastly, reformers and liberal historians of education have been responsible for the American people's failure to understand the true nature and function of schools.[37]

Probably the most extensive revisionist critique is The Great School Legend by Colin Greer. The theme that runs through Professor Greer's book is that the public schools help keep America a country of winners and losers.[38] The faith in the public school, Professor Greer tells us, is sustained through in-house historians whose vested interest is to praise the schools.[39] For Greer there is an elite reality that runs next to the egalitarian rhetoric put out by these in-house historians:

> The ultimate dualism for the school, its elitist reality amid its egalitarian rhetoric, is resolved in the only way it can be, once we assume the constancy of the economic order--by treating erosions in the stated expectation of performance as isolated cultural phenomena. The bootstrap theory is quickly reaffirmed and the plight of those who cannot pull hard enough becomes part of a closely related and equally unresolved dualism in the field of social welfare: The sanctity of every life vs. inconvenience meanwhile, using the bell curve to sustain 19th century Wage Fund Theory (which argued in effect that the industrial world was flat and, therefore, shares infinite), the public school selects winners and losers, more losers than winners, for it is on the effective exclusion of large numbers that the security of an affluent community depends.[40]

Professor Greer tells us that the myth extends to the schooling of the immigrant.[41] Paraphrasing Perkinson's The Imperfect Panacea, he compares it to the schooling of the Black man in American public schools today. The analogy, though, is very shaky. In The Other America, Michael Harrington explains that you cannot understand early twentieth century poverty through an understanding of the poverty of modern times.[42] In the same sense analysis of the Black experience in the public school cannot be transferred to analysis of the early twentieth century immigrant

40

and the public school. As Greer goes on he tells us
that the immigrant who made it did so in spite of the
school. The melting pot, the public school as an
equalizer, and Horatio Alger Jr. and the American dream
are all myth.[43] He cites the number of dropouts and
the failure of the Italians between 1900-1920 as
evidence of the failure of the public school. The only
problem is the success of the Italian second generation
in the late 30's, 40's, and 50's is never mentioned.[44]
The schools were to keep alive a stoicism that made the
immigrant know his place rather than open things up so
that he might live the American dream.[45] Colin Greer
tells us that the only time the immigrant moved up it
was because his labor was needed by the social elite.
The only thing the school could do was to crush the
spirit of the immigrant even as it was looked at as the
great equalizer.[46]

Paul Violas and Clarence Karier look at the
schooling of the immigrant more in terms of social
control under the name of progressivism. Control is
covert and esoteric while the rhetoric is community and
progress. Like Professor Greer, they do not claim
conspiracy but instead allude to the inherent nature of
American capitalism. Violas' "Jane Addams and the New
Liberalism" exemplifies this revisionist thought.
Never denying Miss Addams' humanitarian ideals, Violas
contends that Hull House and the other liberal
progressive reforms are, in the end, softer means of
social control.[47] Jane Addams' work, for Professor
Violas, was to get immigrants to adjust to the social
order: adjust even though it meant killing the essence
of the individual immigrant:[48]

> The problem, however, was to organize and
> direct that force into socially acceptable
> channels. In harmony with the new liberalism
> she helped construct, Miss Addams believed
> the benevolent direction of the masses should
> be controlled by the more intelligent and
> morally superior individuals.[49]

Paul Violas' co-author of Roots of Crisis,
Clarence Karier, equates Jane Addams with John Dewey.
For Professor Karier, John Dewey accepts and advocates
adjustment to the social order at the expense of
individuality.[50] He quotes Dewey on expertise and the
education of the masses by the expert. The claim is
that Dewey's faith was that science would make things
right when used to help society, thus helping the
masses:

41

Although Dewey considered himself a socialist, his were not the concerns of a radical socialist but rather those of a management-welfare state socialist interested in developing and maintaining the system.[51]

Professor Karier, though, sees Dewey's faith as perpetuation of the system through cosmetic changes. The whole of John Dewey is not touched by this interpretation but at the same time Professor Karier hits on the bind that Dewey found himself in. Oftentimes the criticism of Professor Dewey has been that he upheld the individuality of the immigrant. The following words that appeared in The Principle met nationalist opposition:

> The concept of uniformity and unanimity in culture is rather repellent; one cannot contemplate in imagination that every people in the world should talk Volapuk or Esperanto, that the same thoughts should be cultivated, the same beliefs, the same historical traditions, and the same ideals and aspirations for the future. Variety is the spice of life, and the richness and the attractiveness of social institutions depend upon cultural diversity among separate units. In so far as people are all alike, there is no give and take among them. And it is better to give and take.[52]

Now from Professor Karier we are told that it is just the opposite--Professor Dewey, like Hull House and Jane Addams, were tools of social control. The truth might be that Professor Dewey could not separate the individual and the community.[53] School and Society and The Child and the Curriculum argue for the symbiotic relationship of the two elements:

> What the best and wisest parent wants for his own child, that must the community want for all of its children. Any other ideal for our schools is narrow and unlovely; acted upon, it destroys our democracy. All that society has accomplished for itself is put, through the agency of the schools, at the disposal of its future members. All its better thoughts of itself it hopes to realize through the new possibilities thus opened to its future self. Here individualism and

socialism are at one. Only by being true to
the full growth of all the individuals who
make it up, can society by any chance be true
to itself.[54]

A more general critique of the education of the
immigrant is written by Michael Katz in Class,
Bureaucracy, and the Schools. His claim is that
progressive educational reform was a smoke-screen that
clouded the issues and heightened control:[55]

>   Municipal reform represented as much a
>   thrust for power by this group as it did a
>   moral crusade for good government. Bossism,
>   ward politics, and immigrants were linked
>   together in public attitudes. Consequently,
>   an anti-immigrant and anti-working class
>   attitude underlay much of municipal reform.[56]

Katz talks of who the reformers were and then discusses
some of the particular reforms. In general terms his
critique of the reformers and their reforms is that
they are grounded in capitalistic foundations and can
therefore not help but be pawns of the state.[57] He
touches what we have already discussed concerning the
fear of the immigrant:

>   The men and women concerned with altering
>   the control of education had no higher
>   opinion of poor city families than did their
>   predecessors a half century before. They
>   shared the anti-immigrant sentiments and the
>   racism of their class. Insofar as their
>   reform efforts had an educational purpose,
>   that goal again reflected one of the larger
>   aims of municipal reform: the attempt to
>   find new modes of social control appropriate
>   to a dynamic and fluid urban environment.
>   Their aim remained similar to that of earlier
>   reformers; inculcating the poor with
>   acceptable social attitudes. This has had
>   important implications. It has meant that
>   the government of school systems has
>   continued to rest on the disdain for a large
>   portion of students and their families. This
>   has only widened the gulf between working
>   class communities and schools that
>   mid-century reformers had helped to create.
>   Schools remained distant and alien
>   institutions to the poor, the bureaucratic
>   detachment of the staff reinforced by the

43

bias of those in political control of the
system.[58]

Katz turns from this to explain why specific
reforms are both means of control and substantiation of
the status quo. He uses industrial education as an
example of the ushering of a particular class of people
in a direction they wouldn't otherwise choose; all
under the auspices of practical education.[59] For Katz
it was a way to keep workers, workers and bosses,
bosses.

This group of revisionist educators could probably
best be labeled neo-Marxists. They interpret the
education of the immigrant in the early twentieth
century in Marxist terms. As long as the system is
capitalist there is no way in for the immigrant as an
immigrant. Until he becomes a part of the in-class, he
will be treated, and in reality is, the "other". For
the revisionists, the schools are part of the in-class.
Colin Greer, Paul Violas, Clarence Karier, and Michael
Katz have no trouble analyzing the tension in education
that I ponder. Their analysis makes the schools and
equality antithetical--the schools were to control the
immigrant.

Other educational historians see this tension
between social control and equality (melting pot) as
being operative in the schooling of the immigrant.
Some, like Lawrence Cremin, Henry Perkinson, and David
Tyack, speak of the immigrant as they talk about
education in general, others like Maxine Seller and
Mark Krug address the education of the immigrant in
particular.

The Imperfect Panacea by Perkinson and Cremin's
The Transformation of the School both address the
difference between reality and rhetoric. Each tells us
that the schools didn't do all they said they did
towards equality but at the same time they weren't as
bad as the revisionists make them out. Perkinson
concludes that the schools acted more as a selector
than as an equalizer.[60] An equation can be made with
the Thomas Jefferson and W. E. B. Dubois concept of the
talented tenth.[61] Jefferson and Dubois both believed
that through education a natural aristocracy of talent
would rise to the top. In a sense the hope was for an
American version of Plato's philosopher-king.
Jefferson submitted an educational plan in Virginia
called the "Bill for More General Diffusion of
Knowledge." The plan called for the beginning of the

44

common school for all children and the institution of the University of Virginia for higher learning.[62] Jefferson designed the university to be the perfect setting for intellectual endeavors. He really did have a notion of serenity and solitude for thinking and learning. Jefferson believed that without schools the country and its leadership would become stagnant and tyranneous.[63] He knew that restrictions because of wealth meant that we would not have the best possible leadership, thus his plan proposed the common school. Perkinson describes Jefferson's belief in education:

> The identification, cultivation, and preparation of these men of talent became the task of the schools. Jefferson's plan for the state of Virginia clearly embodied this function of selecting and training leaders. His proposed hierarchical educational system would, he declared, rake the best geniuses 'from the rubbish'.[64]

W. E. B. Dubois believed as Jefferson did and he often spoke of Black intellectuals as leaders whose responsibility was the freedom of the Black man. "I believed in the higher education of a Talented Tenth who through their knowledge of modern culture could guide the American Negro into a higher civilization."[65]

Dubois grew up in New Barrington, Massachusetts and was educated at Fisk University, Harvard University, and the University of Berlin. He had tremendous faith in the power of education and he believed that through the common school and the universities the talented tenth would emerge. It would be through this talented tenth that freedom and equality for the Black man would become an American reality. In Souls of Black Folk, Dubois talks of the importance and the success of the Black teacher:

> In a single generation they put thirty thousand black teachers in the south. They wiped out the illiteracy of the majority of the black people of the land, and they made Tuskegee possible.[66]

It is this success that both exemplifies and justifies Dubois' faith in education.

Perkinson includes both Jefferson and Dubois in his analysis of the history of American education and he concludes that the function of the American public school has been to help us determine who is best suited for specific work.[67] The problem is that like father like son is often assumed, thus becoming the reality of the situation. Professor Perkinson talks about Charles Eliot, the President of Harvard University, and the notion of selection:

> Eliot made clear what was happening. All now realized that America was no longer the land of opportunity, in the sense that any man could try his hand at any job. But not everyone realized that this meant that the traditional function of the school must also disappear. Not everyone realized that the schools must give up trying to equalize people and concentrate on working them out for their 'probable destinies'.[68]

Perkinson goes on to say that many educators saw this as an heretical position, denying equality through education. Slogans replaced reality in order to sustain the ideology of equality. In the Imperfect Panacea, selection is somewhere between social control and equality. For Perkinson it is the reality rather than the either/or of the revisionists or the educational sloganeers.[69]

Professor Cremin, the President of the Spencer Foundation, writes of educational reform as something that takes time and has to be treated gently because it is slow. He talks of the meanness of the Americanization of Cubberley and at the same time admires the progressive reform of Jane Addams and John Dewey:[70]

> Local boards were to turn school houses into neighborhood centers for every sort of variety of community activity; the school would be meeting place, public forum, recreation house, civic center, home of all formal and informal education. Ultimately Americanization came to be viewed as a venture in social education, immigrant education as cooperate effort to improve the quality of neighborhood life.[71]

Cremin sees the progressive position in terms of faith in education. Moderate rather than radical, the progressive belief is that the schools, by teaching "truth," will lead to freedom and equality.[72]

Turning Points in American Educational History, by
David Tyack, discusses the tension between control and
equality in the schooling of the early twentieth
century immigrant. Tyack presents material that the
school child had to learn. Included is "The meaning of
Americanization: English for Foreigners," a curriculum
by Sara O'Brien written in the tradition of Cubberley.
Citizenship, grooming, and Anglo-Saxon morality are all
taught as the immigrant learns English.[73] Frank
Thompson would have been proud of the effort.
Professor Tyack also tells us the success stories of
immigrants in the schools. Mary Antin and Leonard
Covello, whom I will discuss later, both knew their
heritage yet both made it as Americans.

But now let's get to two recent works that
specifically discuss the schooling of the immigrant.
Professor Maxine Seller of the State University of New
York at Buffalo and Professor Mark Krug of the
University of Chicago both deal with the concept of the
"melting pot" and the schools.

Maxine Sellers' essay, "Buffalo's Immigrants,"
cites the revisionists, but her analysis tends to go
deeper. Like the revisionists, she feels that money
was misspent, but more faith and less bitterness comes
through her words. She speaks of Americanization and
of the paternalism of educational reformers but she is
able to see both the strength and the beauty of the new
immigrants.[74] Since her study includes only the years
1890-1916, she cites the great success of the Jews in
the schools and the high drop-out rate of Poles and
Italians.[75] Unfortunately, the coming decades which
saw school success by the other groups are not in
Professor Sellers study.[76] What she does capture is
the faith the immigrants had in the schools and their
great desire to be American:

> The native born reformers pursued
> educational goals and programs that reflected
> their own vision of America, sometimes
> coalescing with the needs and desires of the
> immigrant population and sometimes not. With
> the advantages of hindsight, it appears that
> much of the reformers' energies were
> misdirected. Reformers taught patriotism to
> immigrant groups who were already
> passionately devoted to their new homes, and
> middle class virtues to people who were
> already incredibly hardworking, thrifty and
> eager to participate in--not destroy--

47

American capitalism.[77]

A good example of this faith in education comes from Abraham Cahan who was mentioned in the preceding chapter. In his autobiographical work, The Education of Abraham Cahan, he talks of the lengths he went to learn English. Cahan wanted to be American so much he didn't even want to sound foreign.

> In the end I concluded that the best thing for me was to go to school. But if I attended evening school all I would hear would be the speech of other foreigners like myself. I therefore decided that in as much as my daytime hours were free and I did all my teaching in the evenings I would go to a regular public school, together with American Children.[78]

Professor Sellers seems to hit on the truth when she says that the educational reformer did not have to worry about the immigrant learning American ways. The question is, was the faith in the American dream promoted through American education? Is the melting pot a reality and was equality promoted by the schools? Although Moynihan and Glazer disclaim the melting pot, their figures substantiate upward mobility for the Jews and Italians through the schools.[79] At one point eighty-five percent of the students at City College of New York were Jewish. Moynihan and Glazer tell us that this is now down to sixty-five percent because of other colleges opening their doors. They go on to say that for the Jewish immigrant City College was the opener of many new occupational doors. Higher education paid off for the Jewish immigrant.[80] With further examination Moynihan and Glazer conclude that this pattern was followed in the next generation by the Italian immigrant:[81]

> The pattern whereby, among Jews, the children of storekeepers and small businessmen went to college and became professionals, is being repeated, on a smaller scale and generation later, among Italian Americans.[82]

The most recent book that deals with this subject is The Melting of the Ethnics by Mark Krug. This book reviews the literature and weighs the meanness and the beauty of American public education:

Some teachers, by no means all, had little sympathy for the alien immigrant children and were impatient to have them shed their 'foreignness' as soon as possible. On the other hand, as we shall see, many teachers helped and encouraged able immigrant children far beyond the call of duty.[83]

Krug does not deny that the schools and Americanization were often painful but he concludes that American culture is inherently the melting pot. "It would seem that the mainstream culture that confronted the immigrants was not the puritan, Anglo-Saxon culture but an already melted American culture."[84] He finishes the book by discussing, and then quoting, Gunnar Myrdal:

The public schools, the evening schools, and settlement houses played an important role in the absorption of the millions of immigrants. Gunnar Myrdal, the Swedish sociologist, has devoted many years to the study of the American society.[85] In a recent article in The Center Magazine, he made this sound observation on the role of the public schools in the period of large scale immigration:

'Throughout this long period, the immigrants came almost entirely from the lower social and economic strata, in their home countries. All had to start from the bottom and work themselves up; a process aided by the public school system, which, with all its defects, was a relatively efficient vehicle for social mobility, even if it took a generation or two to climb the ladder.'[86]

Mark Krug concludes that the melting pot is a reality and that the public school is one of its essential elements. Krug's study asserts that the immigrants used the facilities of the public school in order to become part of an already melted culture.[87] His argument is exemplified in the discussion that follows.

The Promised Land by Mary Antin and The Heart is the Teacher by Leonard Covello are two autobiographical American dream stories. Each talks of the school as the powerful force. In an essay called "Immigrant Social Aspirations and American Education, 1880-1930,"

Timothy Smith talks of the great faith[88] and vested
interest the immigrant had in education. Professor
Smith tells us that the immigrants wanted to go to
school and made sure that they came away with an
education:

> These aspirations, then the economic, the
> communal, and the civic--propelled immigrants
> from eastern and southern Europe toward (a)
> growing concern for education. Quite as much
> as any coercion from compulsory education
> acts or any pressure from professional
> Americanizers, the immigrant's own hopes for
> his children account for the immense success
> of the public school system.[89]

Mary Antin believed in the schools and believed
they were successful. She was born in Russia and
emigrated to the United States with her family as did
many other Russian Jews. The Promised Land tells of
her life growing up in Boston, Massachusetts. For Mary
Antin, the public school was the savior from the
drudgery of piece work as well as the customs and
superstitions of the old world. She talks about the
great faith she had in the school and also the same
belief of her father. "For a school teacher was no
ordinary mortal in his eyes; she was a superior being,
set above the common run of men by her erudition and
devotion to higher things."[90] Mary Antin felt the
schools and her teachers were devoted to helping her
advance and become the best American woman she could
possibly be. Her ideas and devotions run side by side
with the schools. She talks about the English language
as the language of equality.[91] School is a religious
experience as exemplified by the place she reserves for
George Washington.[92] It's not hard to understand why
the Horatio Alger stories were among Mary Antin's
favorite reading.

We learn in the forward that Mary Antin led a very
successful adult life in New York City. She married
out of the Jewish faith and was prominent along with
her husband in New York City intellectual circles.
Oscar Handlin concludes the forward with an interesting
quote. It typifies the dilemma, or just might be the
saving grace, of the Americanized immigrant:

> She could no more return to the Jewish
> fold than to her mother's womb; but neither
> could she continue to enjoy her accidental
> personal immunity from the penalities of

50

being a Jew in a time of virulent
anti-Semitism. In a moving essay, 'House of
the One Father' (Common Ground, Spring,
1941), she expressed her solidarity with the
people of Polotzk, past and present.[93]

It might be that not only can you not reenter the womb
but neither do you ever totally leave. Roots appear
stronger than we like to admit.

Although different than the life of Mary Antin,
Leonard Covello also signifies the American dream.
Leonard Covello was nine years old when he came to New
York in 1896. Mother and children left their Sicilian
village to join Leonard's father who had come years
earlier to try to pave the way. Leonard's growing up
in America can be equated to Farrel's Horatio Alger
stories. Public school, good grades through study,
jobs both before and after school, led to Covello
getting a Pulitzer scholarship to attend Columbia.
Like Mary Antin, he lauds the teachers, as well as a
woman social worker in the Jane Addams tradition, who
were there when he needed them with aid and
encouragement. For forty-five years Covello was to be
one of those people who aided and encouraged other
immigrants who entered the public schools, first as a
teacher at DeWitt Clinton High and then as principal at
Franklin High School. Leonard Covello never forgot his
roots and his energy was directed to keeping alive the
American dream that was so much a part of his life.

He, too, like Mary Antin, talks of the faith in
the schools of both himself and his father:

Nardo, my father repeated again and
again. In my life you see a dog's life. Go
to school. Even if it kills you. With the
pen and with books you have the chance to
live like a man and not like a beast of
burden.[94]

He goes on to talk of many of his teachers, both good
and bad, of Americanization and the moving upward and
onward of the American dream. And finally what
happened to his school mates as well as many of his
students. Covello really believed that they were his
students. Sixteen hours was a short work day.

One story reaffirms my faith that it is next to
impossible to kill the human spirit, especially the
spirit of a junior high student. Covello talks of a

German teacher he had that, to use the colloquial, was
a "bear":

> You are a rambunctious bunch of bums! he
> would shout, his beard sticking straight out
> at us like the point of a rapier. We had no
> notion of what he was saying but the sound
> delighted us. Rambunctious bums! we yelled
> to each other. One boy, I remember, was so
> amused by the sound of German that he leapt
> out of his seat and into the aisle, holding
> his belly, convulsed with laughter, while
> poor Hofstadter blustered and turned red in
> the face.[95]

But this was the exception. Teachers were looked up to
because they represented what it was to be American.
And American is what immigrant children wanted to be.
Covello understood that this was often at the expense
of friends and family:

> Our teachers impressed us mainly because
> they did not live in the neighborhood. They
> dressed better and spoke differently and
> seemed to come from somewhere beyond the
> horizon. Somehow we tried to measure up to
> this outer world which we knew as American,
> though we had no conception of what it was.
> Only its people had a life for and with
> greater luxuries than ours. But in trying to
> make a good impression on our teachers, it
> was always at the expense of our family and
> what was Italian in us.[96]

Leonard Covello thought it was important to keep track
of the lives of his students after they left the public
school. Covello concludes <u>The Heart is the Teacher</u>
very pleased. Great numbers of his students, like
himself, were living the American dream. As teacher
and principal he was very pleased that the public
school that he had devoted his life to had helped along
many young immigrants, Leonard Covello included.

Interestingly enough as I began interviewing
people in Cleveland I was introduced to a modern day
Leonard Covello. Vince Julian was born in this
country--the son of an Italian immigrant. In Italy his
father was a sheepherder and in this country he was a
foundry worker. Julian grew up next to the foundry in
New Castle, Pennsylavania. He remembers the foundry
well and both he and his father knew that he was to

have a different life. Julian said that there never had to be direct conversation, it was assumed that he would wear a tie and jacket. He taught social studies and is now principal of Bellfaire School in Cleveland. many of the thoughts Covello had on education were repeated by Vince Julian when we spoke. Like Covello, Vince Julian is an example of the American dream and he works to keep it open for his students.

The Horatio Alger stories of Leonard Covello and Mary Antin or the ideology of social control do not answer the question of the schooling of the immigrant and the melting pot. While the revisionist ideology is harsh and unconvincing, two autobiographical Horatio Alger stories do not insure the school as the equalizer for the immigrant. In Class, Bureaucracy, and Schools, Michael Katz says, "Even if we grant that a number of innovations entered school rooms and school systems, we still must ask about more fundamental issues."[97] Katz goes on to assume that we would find out that the immigrants were treated poorly by the schools. But Katz assumed that before he asked for deeper addressing of fundamental issues. It is in this deeper addressing of fundamental issues that I stand with Michael Katz. The question of how the school affected the immigrants still remains unresolved. Chapter 4 will study the lives of Jewish immigrants who attended American public schools. Hopefully we might come away with deeper understanding of the schooling of the immigrant.

Footnotes

[1]Horace Mann, Lectures on Education (Boston: Ide and Cutton, 1855), pp. 71-72.

[2]Henry Perkinson, The Imperfect Panacea (New York: Random House, 1968), p. 70.

[3]Ibid.

[4]Herold, The American Faith in the Schools as an Agency of Progress: Promise and Fulfillment, pp. 1-12.

[5]Ibid., p. 7.

[6]For clarification, see Goldman, Rendezvous With Destiny, Chapter 4.

[7]Richard Hofstadter, Social Darwinism in American Thought (Boston: Beacon Press, 1955), pp. 56-68.

[8]Ibid., p. 58.

[9]Ibid.

[10]Ibid., p. 66.

[11]Ibid., pp. 81-82.

[12]Ibid., p. 82.

[13]Ibid., p. 84.

[14]Ibid.

[15]Richard Nelson, "The Pathological Model and the Schools: A critical Inquiry" (unpublished Ph.D. dissertation, The Ohio State University, 1975), pp. 1-5.

[16]Robert Hunter, Poverty in Reforming American Life in the Progressive Era, ed. by H. Landon Warner (New York: Pitman, 1971), p. 51.

[17]Ibid.

[18]Nelson, The Pathological Model and the Schools: A Critical Inquiry, pp. 123.

[19]Ibid.

[20]Ibid.

[21]Jane Addams, Democracy and Social Ethics (New York: MacMillan, 1907), pp. 228-237.

[22]Ibid.

[23]Mehl, Classic Educational Ideas, p. 210.

[24]Ellwood P. Cubberley, Changing Conceptions of Education (Boston: Houghton Mifflin Co., 1909), p. 15.

[25]Ibid.

[26]Ibid.

[27]Ibid., pp. 64-68.

[28]Ibid.

[29]Frank V. Thompson, Schooling of the Immigrant (New York: Harper and Brothers, 1920), p. 74.

[30]Sartre, Anti-Semite and Jew, p. 53.

[31]Ibid., p. 27.

[32]Ibid., p. 54.

[33]W. J. Cash, The Mind of the South, pp. 68-81.

[34]Ibid.

[35]Thompson, Schooling of the Immigrant, pp. 74-76.

[36]Ibid.

[37]Diane Ravitch, The Revisionists Revised: Studies in the Historiography of American Education (New York: National Academy of Education, 1977), pp. 8-9. (Was republished by Basic Books, 1978)

[38]Colin Greer, The Great School Legend (New York: Basic Books, 1972), p. 37.

[39]Ibid., pp. 37-59.

[40]Ibid., p. 37.

[41]Ibid., p. 83.

[42]Harrington, The Other America, pp. 1-19.

[43]Greer, The Great School Legend, p. 88.

[44]Moynihan and Glazer, Beyond the Melting Pot, pp. 204-205.

[45]Greer, The Great School Legend, pp. 60-79.

[46]Ibid., p. 88.

[47]Paul Violas, "Jane Addams and the New Liberalism" in Roots of Crisis: American Education in the Twentieth Century (Chicago: Rand McNally and Co., 1973), p. 83.

[48]Ibid., p. 81.

[49]Ibid.

[50]Clarence Karier, "Liberal Ideology and the Quest for Orderly Change," in Roots of Crisis: American Education in the Twentieth Century (Chicago: Rand McNally and Co., 1973), pp. 101-104.

[51]Ibid., p. 92.

[52]Dewey, The Principle, pp. 205-206.

[53]Dewey, The School and Society, p. 7.

[54]Ibid.

[55]Michael B. Katz, Class, Bureaucracy, and Schools (New York: Praeger Publishers, 1973), pp. 114-125.

[56]Ibid., p. 115.

[57]Ibid., pp. 114-125.

[58]Ibid., p. 116.

[59]Ibid., pp. 120-123.

[60]Henry Perkinson, The Imperfect Panacea (New York: Random House, 1958), pp. 145-146.

[61]Ibid., pp. 51-55, 145-146.

[62]Charles Flinn Arrowood, Thomas Jefferson and Education in a Republic (New York: McGraw-Hill, 1930), pp. 49-79.

[63] Ibid.

[64] Perkinson, The Imperfect Panacea, pp. 9-10.

[65] W. E. Burghardt Dubois, Dusk of Dawn (New York: Schocken Books, 1968), p. 70.

[66] Dubois, Souls of Black Folks (New York: Fawcett Publications, 1961), pp. 79-80.

[67] Perkinson, The Imperfect Panacea, pp. 144-146.

[68] Ibid., p. 146.

[69] Ibid.

[70] Lawrence A. Cremin, The Transformation of the School (New York: Alfred Knopf, 1961), pp. 60-75, 347-353.

[71] Ibid., p. 75.

[72] Ibid., p. 89.

[73] David Tyack, Turning Points in American Educational History (Waltham, Mass.: Blaisdell Publishing Co., 1967), pp. 239-243.

[74] Maxine Seller, "The Education of Immigrant Children in Buffalo, New York 1890-1916," New York History, April, 1976, pp. 195-198.

[75] Ibid.

[76] Moynihan and Glazer, Beyond the Melting Pot, pp. 204-205.

[77] Seller, "The Education of Immigrant Children in Buffalo, New York 1890-1916," p. 198.

[78] Cahan, The Education of Abraham Cahan, p. 239.

[79] Moynihan and Glazer, Beyond the Melting Pot, pp. 204-205.

[80] Ibid.

[81] Ibid., p. 206.

[82] Ibid., p. 206.

[83]Mark Krug, The Melting of the Ethnics (Bloomington, Indiana: Phi Delta Kappa Educational Foundations, 1976), p. 88.

[84]Ibid., p. 99.

[85]Myrdal's most famous and comprehensive work is The American Dilemma.

[86]Ibid., p. 103.

[87]Ibid., pp. 95-104.

[88]Timothy Smith, "Immigrant Social Aspirations and American Education," Education in American History (New York: Praeger, 1973), p. 250.

[89]Ibid.

[90]Mary Antin, The Promised Land (Boston: Houghton Mifflin Co., 1969), p. 217.

[91]Ibid., p. 208.

[92]Ibid., p. 223.

[93]Ibid., p. xiv.

[94]Leonard Covello, The Heart is the Teacher (New York: McGraw-Hill, 1958), p. 41.

[95]Ibid., p. 43.

[96]Ibid., p. 47.

[97]Katz, Class, Bureaucracy, and Schools, p. 120.

CHAPTER 4

THE SCHOOLING OF THE IMMIGRANTS--
INTERVIEWS WITH JEWISH IMMIGRANTS

I suspect the preacher spoke for the people in this book, too. In their rememberings are their truths. The precise fact or the precise date is of small consequence. This is not a lawyer's brief nor an annotated sociological treatise. It is simply an attempt to get the story of the holocaust known as The Great Depression from an improvised battalion of survivors!1

This paragraph is found in the book Hard Times by Studs Terkel. The people he interviews in Hard Times; as well as in his other books, Division Street: America, Working, and American Dreams; come alive for the reader. You feel that you have met each person. At the same time there is a knowledge of the time or subject of each book. The depression becomes much clearer after reading Hard Times just as Working helps the reader understand the feelings and aspirations of both the coal miner and the business executive. Terkel's books are filled with the words of many people. Both famous people and ordinary folk whose recorded words are now called oral history. By interviewing immigrants who attended the public school, by doing oral history, we get a clearer picture of the schools and the immigrant.

Many essays on oral history have appeared in history journals in the last decade. Historians spend time writing rejoinders at each other arguing the validity of the discipline. There are true believers who spend a great deal of time writing justification against hard line historians who think that interviews are nice but not as history.2 This gentle criticism was repeated by Dr. Nathan Reingold in a paper, entitled "A Critic Looks at Oral History," that he delivered at the Fourth National Colloquium on Oral History:

Dr. Och said to me over the phone he thought that when the association had conventional historians here in the past or in the other situations, they were rather condescending about oral history. That is, they said, 'Oh well, you get a few opinions in retrospect and the nice local anecdotes

59

sort of thing. This is very pleasant to have
but obviously not very important.'[3]

But the question that has to be asked is why are
the opinions and the lives of everyday people any less
important than the opinions and the lives of those
people in high places? Why is one "real history: and
the other "pleasant but obviously not very important"?
In The Political Illusion, Jacques Ellul argues that we
deceive ourselves and give validity to things that are
not substantial. In the following paragraph he
discusses politics--an anology can be made to history:

We consider it obvious that everything
must be unreservedly subjected to the power
of the state; it would seem extraordinary to
us if any activity should escape it. The
expansion of the state's encroachment upon
all affairs is exactly paralleled by our
conviction that things must be that way. Any
attempt on the part of any enterprise,
university, or charitable enterprise to
remain independent of the state seems
anachronistic to us. The state directly
incarnates the common zeal. The state is the
great ordainer, the great organizer, the
center upon which all voices of all people
converge and from which all reasonable,
balanced, impartial--i.e., just--solutions
emerge. If by chance we find this not so, we
are profoundly scandalized, so filled are we
with this image of the state's perfection.
In our current consciousness no other center
of decision in our social body can exist. To
repeat: it is not just the fact of the state
being at the center of our lives that is
crucial, but our spontaneous and personal
acceptance of it as such. We believe that
for the world to be in good order, the state
must have all the powers.[4]

Just as Ellul finds this an illusion, it is an
illusion to think that history exists only on a higher
level than everyday man. Oral history is a choice to
study history where it exists...in the lives of every
man.

Allan Nevins is probably the historian who has
devoted the most time and pages to oral history as a
discipline. He was involved in setting up oral history
programs at Columbia University and at the University

60

of California at Berkeley. Professor Nevins has
written on oral history in The Gateway to History and
Allen Nevins on History. The first book was written in
1938. Interviews as history is not a new phenomena.
Often reference is made to Thucydides, as the first
oral historian, in the fifth century B.C. Washington
journalist Ellie Abel tells us that Thucydides warned
us of the shortcomings of the discipline:[5] "The task
was a laborious one because eye witnesses of the same
occurrence gave accounts of them as they remembered or
were interested in the actions of one side or the
other."[6] Although oral history is not new, Professor
Nevins stresses its modern day importance because of
the technological age in which we live. He thinks that
oral history can save antiquity that now dies because
we no longer write letters which were at one time very
personal historical documents. Louis Starr, former
director of the Columbia University Oral Research
Office, makes the same point:

> The automobile, the airliner, and the
> telephone between them are steadily
> obliterating history's most treasured
> resource, the confidential letter. The inner
> thoughts, the private revelations, the
> reactions of one man to another, the
> undercurrent of the times as reflected in our
> personal lives, will be lost to him (the
> historian) simply because we no longer
> confide to one another in writing as earlier
> generations did. As the vernacular has it,
> we contact one another, be it by car, plane
> or phone. We talk.[7]

It is the recording of this talk that Nevins
believes breathes fresh air into history. Human
personality makes for delightful reading and gives us
new insight into our historical roots. But like any
other discipline there are still arguments and
divisions within the field. Most historians accept
oral history as "real" history, but of course there are
still those that claim that it is invalid. In an
article titled "The Literature of Oral History,"
Professor Donald Schippers of UCLA writes about staunch
oral history critic, Professor Fred Shannon.

> Professor Shannon, the chief critic, in
> a remarkably short time assessed oral history
> as almost totally worthless. Working on the
> assumption that most oral history memoirs
> consist of the reminiscences of garrulous old

men, he assailed the process on the basis
that, first, no memory source is reliable
and, second, that the information obtained is
too trivial to be significant, anyway.[8]

Professor Shannon, though, is the extreme critic
and has to be treated as such. Logically, the same
faults he finds with oral history can be found with the
documents, letters, etc. that make up "real" history.
They have to come under the same scrutiny. But this is
not to just put it off, within the field there is still
room for questions and discussion.

One question that is often asked is how to know
truth from lie? In a panel discussion at the Second
National Colloquium on Oral History, William
Leuchtenburg of Columbia University warned that
although there is no way to be sure of validity, the
oral historian has to proceed carefully:

> Especially one has to remember that in a
> memoir or in an autobiography, the person
> giving the memoir is the hero of the story,
> and one has to be careful in assessing his
> presentation of how important he was to any
> historical event. One has to remember, too,
> that as the hero of the story, he is going to
> reconstruct history, not necessarily by
> lying, not by deliberate falsification, but
> in order to present his position in the best
> historical light.[9]

Leuchtenburg goes on to suggest that what the oral
historian has to do is become aware of the
consistencies or inconsistencies in his interviews.
Obviously there will be mistakes, but there will also
be a tremendous wealth of information.[10]

Another issue is the argument between spontaneity
and formalism. What is the function of the
interviewer? For Terkel, the interviewer is a listener
and spontaneity is the key to good work. Two other
oral historians, Elizabeth Rumics and Helen McCann
White, stress the importance of organization:

> An oral history project comprises an
> organized series of interviews with selected
> individuals or groups in order to create new
> source materials from the reminiscences of
> their own life and acts, or from their
> association with a particular person, period,

or event.[11]

Gould P. Colman goes further and stresses formal training and certification for the oral historian. The issue, though, is not one of either/or. Spontaneity does not deny the listener being knowledgeable in the subject of the interview. It is not synonymous with chaos. At the same time, organization should not mean that the interviewer is not flexible depending on the particular situation. Since the interview is conducted to understand the life and times of the person interviewed, it seems only sensible that there be limits to both positions. It is within these limits that the interview occurs.

The function and the beauty of oral history is probably discussed best in "Reflections on Oral History" by Saul Benison. Without denying the problems and the divisions, he cuts through them in order not to trivialize history. The man in the street is history and Professor Benison knows that his story is history's responsibility if history is in fact a search for truth:

> We learn about these people from what others write or say about them; they rarely speak for themselves to historians. We make inferences about them, we deal with them as groups, but basically, we don't know them as people except in those rare instances when someone records the eloquence of a Chief Joseph or Nat Turner. Their tradition is basically an oral tradition that lives within the family group or the locality for a generation or two and then slowly disappears. Paradoxically, oral historians can make an important contribution to an understanding of recent American history by gathering the autobiographies and life histories of immigrants who came to the United States in the early twentieth century or of industrial or farm workers or of Negroes. When I mention these groups, I do not mean their leaders--I mean them.[12]

Professor Benison's call to oral history is the basic approach taken in this phase of the study. Each person interviewed was asked a schedule of planned questions. The questions were a starting point, and the hope was that those interviewed would "open up" with their stories. In most cases this was no problem;

63

the people interviewed were anxious to tell their
stories. Immigration, the experience of the immigrant
in the school, and the lives of their children and
grandchildren are included in the interviews. The
following questions comprised the interview schedule:

1. What country did you come from?
2. Why did you leave?
3. What year did you come and how old were you
   when you came?
4. Did you go to school in Europe?
5. Who did you come to this country with?
6. When did you start school in the United
   States?
7. What grade did you start in?
8. What was the attitude towards school at
   home?
9. What was your father's occupation? Mother's
   occupation?
10. What language was spoken at home?
11. How was religion treated at home?
12. What are your memories of learning English in
    school?
13. Do you remember any particular subjects being
    stressed?
14. What do you remember about teachers?
15. How were your grades?
16. How long did you attend school?
17. Did you graduate?
18. What did you do after you left school?
19. What was the function of the school? Did it
    succeed?
20. Did the school help or hurt the "American
    dream"?
21. How far did your children and grandchildren
    go in school?
22. What do they do for a living?
23. Where do they live today?
24. Is Judaism as strong today as when you first
    came to the U.S.?
25. Did the public school affect your life?

It is from these questions that the immigrants
spoke of their school memories. There are questions to
be asked concerning methodology and oral history in
general. Are the interviews objective or subjective?
Why these questions? Why were these people interviewed
and not others? And finally, are interviews valid
research (the perils of memory)? The questions are not
posed to initiate debate, just as the interviews were
not recorded to say this is "the way it was," they said

it, and their words are gospel. Rather, the interviews are summarized and presented in this chapter in order to supplement the history analyzed in the first two chapters. Henry Resnick put it well in his review of Hard Times. The review was titled, "When American Was Singing, Buddy Can You Spare A Dime?":

> As long as the proponents of oral history and tape recorded literature do not try to claim inherently greater truth for their work than that of any other historical or literary form, the question of editorial technique is a minor one. The real significance of the new form rests in the liberating effect it can have on speech and language and the human trutch to which it frequently leads. At a time when language and words are all too often utilitarian tools, our culture desperately needs this new approach.[13]

It was with this in mind that the following interviews were recorded. Not with a didactic this-was-the-way-it-was, but rather with the hopes of adding to the understanding of the public school, the immigrant, and twentieth century America.

The interviews were with Jewish immigrants in Cleveland, Ohio. The people interviewed came to the United States between 1895 and 1923. As has been mentioned before, the people that came to the United States during this time period are referred to as the "new immigrants". The selection of the Jewish immigrant does not necessarily tell the story of the school experiences of other immigrant groups. The hope is that trends found in the Jewish experience can stand next to and maybe initiate the same kind of work with other immigrant groups. This work is not done to deny but rather to accompany the work already being[14] undertaken with school records and census tracts. Over thirty people were interviewed and thirteen of those interviews are summarized on the following pages.

Rae Davis

Rae Davis came to Cleveland, Ohio from Russia in
1920. She was six years old and the journey was made
with her mother and two sisters. Like many other
immigrant families, they met her father who had
preceded them to this country. He left Russia because
he had no intentions of serving in the Czar's army.
This seems to be one of the prominent reasons for
Jewish emigration from Russia at that time. In
Cleveland, her dad was a butcher; he also went to night
school to learn English. Rae was sent to public school
as soon as the family arrived in Cleveland. There was
no questions in anyone's mind, in America public school
was where Jewish immigrants sent their children.

Mrs. Davis' first memory is the special English
classes for immigrant children. The classes were
called "steamer classes" after the steam ships that
brought the immigrants to the United States. Mrs.
Davis remembers the "steamer class" being a painless
experience. The teacher was patient and really wanted
to convey the language to the immigrant children.
Observation was stressed. This class as well as
mingling with the other children helped her to learn
English very quickly. This, though, did not erase the
fact that some other children picked on her and other
immigrant children. Being called a greenhorn was not
uncommon but neither were the effects overwhelming. As
far as English goes, it has to be remembered that her
dad was also speaking and learning the language. Mrs.
Davis remembers telling her mother, "you are
reverting," when her mother spoke Yiddish instead of
English in the home. She quickly added that her mother
wanted to speak English--Americans spoke English.

Besides the "steamer class", three teachers from
grammar school were remembered as being excellent.
There were no teachers that were awful and most were
neither good nor bad. Mrs. Woldman stands out because
she taught Mrs. Davis how to write. Penmanship is
mentioned over and over again in the interviews.
Penmanship included grammar and punctuation as well as
the mechanics of writing style. It was a skill to be
mastered and Mrs. Woldman encouraged and taught this
mastery. A second teacher, Miss Wonderlick, believed
in the "school without walls" before the term was
coined. Movies, the public library, and the corner ice
cream parlor were all included in her curriculum. Mrs.

Davis said that Miss Wonderlick lived for her students. Mrs. Davis' sixth grade teacher, Miss Bowmer, also had this commitment and involvement with her students. The classroom was a comfortable place. More interesting, Mrs. Davis remembers the whole class invading Miss Bowmer's home on more than one occasion. I stress the whole class because it was not a reward for good students, but genuine concern for the class as a whole.

After grammar school, Mrs. Davis went to Patrick Henry Junior High and Glenville High School. She graduated from Glenville in 1931. At Glenville she took an academic major to prepare her for college. Her major course of study was French and she remembers the teacher, Miss Rogoff, as both competent and encouraging. A high school English teacher is remembered because the students were afraid of her. Mrs. Davis had to qualify it by saying that she knew her stuff.

Education was an important part of Mrs. Davis' life. The school and the family both promoted learning. Books, Nancy Drew and Louisa May Alcott, stood out and reading was encouraged at school. High school graduation was hopefully a ticket to college. Mrs. Davis had good grades, the grading scale was: E--excellent, G--good, F--fair, D--failing. Unfortunately, many dreams and aspirations were foregone by Americans because of the depression. Mrs. Davis did graduate from high school, but college became and impossibility. She helped her dad out for awhile and then worked as a secretary until she got married. She is again a secretary today. The interesting thing is that without the penmanship, the grammar, and the English she learned in school, her work would have been in a factory, not an office. For the immigrant, office work was a step up.

Mr. Davis grew up in West Virginia. He, too, graduated from high school and he was a businessman in Cleveland. There are three daughters who all live in Cleveland. Two have families and the youngest daughter is single and works. The oldest daughter went to Ohio State University for a year and a quarter before she got married. The second daughter graduated from Kent State University and taught school in Cleveland.

Mrs. Davis' father stressed education and learning was part of the home as well as the school. The public school in Cleveland opened up learning and gave Mrs. Davis an education she couldn't have otherwise experienced. There is no great debt in Mrs. Davis' tone, but there is respect for both the school and the teacher. She followed her father and stressed the importance of schooling for her daughters. The school was for learning and it did its job.

Selma Monosson

Selma Monosson came to Sharon, Pennsylvania, from
Russia on Thanksgiving Day, 1913. She flunked out of
the Russian gymnasium when she was ten years old.
Memories of the gymnasium are anything but fond. She
remembers Jewish students committing suicide because
they had flunked out. Religious discrimination was
common practice.

Miss Monosson was eleven years old when her father
took her to school in Sharon. Her father had begun
studying English on the boat and it was of prime
importance. One of the reasons they came to the United
States was so their children could go to school. There
was no future in Russia. The family was already a
secular family but being anti-religious and
anti-zionistic did not mean you were accepted in
Russia. You were and always would be Jewish. At
school, Miss Monosson was placed in first grade. She
got special attention because her cousins who preceded
her were bright and the teachers assumed the same of
her. This was good in some ways, but it also meant
certain expectations she could not meet. It took Miss
Monosson about three years to learn English. Both the
school and the home were forces that affected her
youth. Books and English and being a self-sustaining
American were values stressed both at home and at
school. Inspiration at home might have spurred getting
the tools at school. There were bad teachers, but
there were also teachers that genuinely inspired their
students academically.

Miss Monosson believed that the main reason to go
to school was to obtain the knowledge necessary to have
a profession. It was important to be able to stand on
your own and the school provided her with this ability.
Her grades were average and she graduated from high
school when she was nineteen. Her sister who was eight
years younger graduated from high school and then
Oberlin College. One interesting aside is that Miss
Monosson spoke English with an Irish accent. The
school was almost entirely Irish.

After graduation, Miss Monosson wanted to become a
nurse. In order to please her dad, she instead
enrolled in Indiana State (P.A.) Normal School to
become a teacher. She really wanted to be a nurse, so
she left in 1924 to study at Mt. Sinai School of

Nursing in New York. She was there until 1928 when she left for St. Louis where she worked as a nurse for many years. She was involved in children's clinics, V.D. and birth control clinics and finally, a tuberculosis clinic. She talked of many Jewish immigrants having TB because of their sweatshop jobs.

Miss Monosson came to Cleveland during World War II. She had relatives here and she still works as a nurse today. She really believes that the public school provided the knowledge that helped her to be a free, independent, American woman. The education is part of the freedom which she was denied in Russia.

Nathan Lev

    Nathan Lev's experience in the public school or
his life in general is far from the typical immigrant
experience.   Peddler,   teacher,   businessman,   and
student; all are part of Mr. Lev's eighty-seven years.
Education has been a part of every one of those years.
He was born in Lutzin, Russia, in 1891 and came to the
United States when he was thirteen and a half.   In
Russia   he   attended   Cheder   and   public   school
simultaneously.   In Cheder, the Bible, the Talmud, and
commentary by Rashi were the curriculum.   Learning was
not a means-ends endeavor.   You studied for the sake of
study.   The second Cheder teacher stands out as having
possibly the greatest effect of all his teachers.   It
was Mr. Yenkell's love of people, his teaching came
from his heart.   The secular school was called Jewish
School.   It was a secular school set up by the
government and it was the school Jews were compelled to
attend.   Nothing in the curriculum was Jewish and the
teachers were men without a home.   They were Jewish,
but did not practice, and at the same time they were
not accepted as Russians.

    Mr. Lev came to his brother in Chicago in 1904.
His brother took him to Foster School.   Since he did
not speak English, he was put in first grade where he
stayed for three or four months.   The school was mostly
Jewish and the teachers were more often than not
Protestant.   Their job was to make you American as
quickly as possible and it was American that the
immigrants wanted to become.   Mr. Lev said that the
teachers were the same as they have been at all times,
some were good, some were bad, and most were
nondescript either way.   School came very easily and
just as he was deeply interested in language in Russia,
he was interested in America, only here the language
was English.   From grammar school one teacher stands
out.   Mrs. Catlin was actually the principal of the
school.   Mr. Lev remembers her spending time with him
on numerous occasions.   In particular, he remembers her
helping him with decimals in the fifth grade.   He had
never had them and the class he had joined already knew
so Mrs. Catlin took time from her day to help Mr. Lev
catch up.   Times were hard though and Mr. Lev had to
work as well as go to school.   His first job began when
he was fifteen.   He worked cataloging for a directory
publisher and both reading and writing English were
essential.   Mr. Lev graduated from grammar school and

he wanted to go to high school. Finding a job was not easy and his sister talked him into coming to Cleveland. She knew that her brother wanted to continue his education very badly and she thought he might find it easier to get work in Cleveland. She had gone to normal school and was a teacher. She and her husband helped Mr. Lev out, but it was still necessary for him to find work. After typical odd jobs, Mr. Lev got a job teaching Hebrew at what is now Heights Temple. The pay was forty dollars a month and the job was in the late afternoon. Mr. Lev enrolled in Central High School the morning after he got the job.

Mr. Lev's first recollection of high school is a placement test of sorts. He met the principal who sent him to see Miss Adams, the head of the English department. She asked him if he knew Julius Caesar. When the answer was yes, he was told to write an encyclopedic essay in ten minutes. It was on the merit of this exercise that they had Mr. Lev enroll in Central High School as a sophomore. Central was about thirty percent Jewish, fifteen percent Black, and the rest White Anglo-Saxon. Mr. Lev's memory is of an harmonious atmosphere. He helped form a Jewish history club which he described as a club of secular Yiddishkite. Like grammar school, most of the teachers were rather ordinary. Three teachers stand out from high school. One stands out because of his incompetency and the other two because of their competence. The first was an English teacher who spent five days a week listening to passages that the students had to memorize. Mr. Lev recalls that the teacher found a way to make Hamlet boring. Mr. Lev's Latin teacher was Foster Lewis. He remembers him as a teacher with a great sense of humor who also taught his students Latin. The teacher Mr. Lev remembers as being outstanding was Miss Adams. She was the same woman who gave him the test on Julius Caesar. Miss Adams taught senior English. She made literature a part of her students and her students a part of the literature she taught. Literature and life were one in the same, Shakespeare was not an abstraction.

Mr. Lev graduated from Central and enrolled in Adelbert College which is now part of Case Western Reserve University. By this time he was principal of the Hebrew school. Along with that job, he began teaching night school for the Cleveland Board of Education. Most of his students were immigrants who wanted to learn English, but had to work during the day. This was followed each night by tutoring students in English. Three lessons cost a dollar.

I'm tempted to stop right here, but Mr. Lev's life
as a teacher and a student is still going on today. He
quit Adelbert and opened a school to teach immigrants
English.   I asked him about quitting and he said that
the degree just wasn't the important thing. After the
school, he opened a book and art store called
Garber-Lev Book and Art Company.   This, too, ran its
time and he opened a business called Ohio Stationary
which his sons still run today. Again the story seems
like it should end, but it doesn't. At fifty-seven, he
turned the business over to his sons and he enrolled in
Columbia University to study literature.   He stayed
there for three years and then became a student and
teacher at the New School of Social Research where he
stayed for a quarter of a century.

Mr. Lev will always be a teacher and a student.
The question of the effect of school and the American
dream could not be asked; he does not think in those
terms.

Gertrude Paston

Mrs. Paston came to Cleveland in 1921. Her dad had come from Poland in 1911. She followed with her mother and two brothers. She was ten years old. Of course her father spoke English and one of the first things he did when the family arrived was to take her to public school. Yiddish was spoken in the home, but everyone wanted to speak English very badly. Her first experience was rather traumatic, but in retrospect, she views public school as a very good experience. Mrs. Paston was a very tall and skinny ten-year-old, but since she couldn't speak English, she was put in the kindergarten class. She was too tall to fit into the kindergarten desk so they had to move Mrs. Paston to the first grade. Seems like a sound pedagogical move. Mrs. Paston was only in the first grade for one semester and then she moved rapidly through elementary and junior high school. No particular teacher is remembered but rather a general tolerance and compassion between teacher and student. Like many of the other people I have spoken with, Mrs. Paston mentioned the stress placed on penmanship, grammar, and English in general. There was tremendous encouragement from teachers in these subjects.

Respect for the teacher and wanting to speak English and be American were forces at home. Her home was kosher, but Mrs. Paston's family was not orthodox. The importance of English is exemplified by her mother enrolling in night school to learn the language. Mrs. Paston was in junior high at the time and she went with her mother and took notes so that her mother could study at home.

Mrs. Paston said that the school helped to understand the great diversity that makes America. Self-sufficiency as an American was much easier because of the public school. After junior high, Mrs. Paston went to business school with the promise of a job that was never to come. She worked at a department store until she got married. Mr. Paston had a dry cleaning store and then a men's haberdashery. Like her mother, Mrs. Paston kept a kosher home and went to temple on the high holidays. The Pastons had one son. He graduated from Glenville High School and Case Tech. He is an engineer for IBM in Endicott, New York. He has three sons. The oldest boy is a paramedic. The middle son is ready to begin college and will study photography; and interestingly enough, the youngest son who is sixteen goes to the Jewish Academy rather than public school.

Rae Sherman

    Rae Sherman came to the United States with her
mother and five brothers and sisters. They met her
father who was already in Chicago, Illinois. Mrs.
Sherman was only two years old when the family came.
As soon as she was old enough, she was taken to school.
This was in spite of her father being a Rabbi. Public
school was the thing you did and her family was no
different. In the home Yiddish was spoken; her father
spoke English, but her mother stuck to Yiddish.

    Mrs. Sherman began grammar school when she was
five years old. In what seems to be common practice,
she went through eighth grade and then went to work.
Completion of eighth grade meant that you were a
grammar school graduate. Mrs. Sherman was not a
rigorous student, but she enjoyed and profited from
school. Mrs. Sherman recalls the importance of
penmanship. Writing was stressed in school and she was
encouraged to work on this skill. Neatness, correct
grammar, and written language in general appear to be
the ticket out of sweatshop piecework. It meant a more
respected, better paying, and easier job for Mrs.
Sherman.

    Besides the practical aspects, she remembers the
school as a great lesson in social America. The school
was a mixture of many ethnic cultures and Mrs. Sherman
remembers both teachers and students mixing well. She
felt that the "American dream" was a reality. Only one
particular teacher stands out in Mrs. Sherman's public
school experience. Most of her teachers were patient
and competent, but she remembers a fourth grade teacher
who was intolerant and had no feeling for the children.
Mrs. Sherman adds that the school knew it and the
teacher was terminated after just one year.

    Like many other Jewish children, Mrs. Sherman went
to Hebrew school each day after public school let out.
An interesting point is that the things she learned in
Hebrew school were soon forgotten; she was American and
public school, not Yiddishkite, was reinforced by her
day to day experience. Grammar school ended when Mrs.
Sherman was thirteen and that meant finding a job.
Like Rae Davis, Rae Sherman did office work until she
was married at sixteen. She was a receptionist and
office clerk and she had no intentions of working in a
factory or sweatshop.

    She met Mr. Sherman when she was sixteen and they

had two children. Mr. Sherman came to the United States from Ireland. He was an entertainer for a short time and then a businessman. The Sherman's daughter is a social worker in Cleveland. She went to the University of Illinois and took a master's degree at Western Reserve. Mrs. Sherman said that she was always a good student and that college was never in question. There are also three grandchildren. Two girls, one goes to nursing school in Columbus, and the other is studying architecture at Ohio Northern. Mrs. Sherman's grandson graduated from Ohio State and is an accountant in Cleveland. The Sherman's son is named Bobby Sherman and he is a comedian in Florida and New York. He plays Florida in the winter and the Catskills in the summer. He graduated from high school, but voice, acting, and dancing lessons went along with the public school.

Mrs. Sherman believes in the public school. For herself and her family the school provided the education and training to be part of America.

Sarah Greenbaum

Sarah Greenbaum came to the lower east side of New York in 1907. She was four years old and she came with her mother and five brothers and sisters. Her father was already here; he worked as a carpenter. A year later she was in school and learning English. Her dad spoke English, but Yiddish was the language in the home. At the same time the school, and especially the teacher, were given reverence in the home. The Jewish concept of the teacher as a rabbi was transferred to the public school teacher.

Mrs. Greenbaum went to school in New York and then went to Case Woodland School in Cleveland. She graduated from the eighth grade and her finest reflection was that she learned English in the school. The school taught the basic curriculum of reading, writing, and arithmetic. She felt that these subjects were taught well in the school, but neither was she excited nor did any teacher excite her with school subjects. She said that she did not do well and did not really care too much about doing well. Graduating from grammar school was expected, so she graduated. High school was never even considered. Mrs. Greenbaum's dad sent to business school with the hope that it would prepare her for office work. She did not like it any more than she liked public school. She said that she just was not a student. An interesting thing is that along with public school, she went to Jewish school on weekends. The curriculum included arts and crafts and for Mrs. Greenbaum it was enjoyment. She liked working with her hands and producing a product. Mrs. Greenbaum quit business school and got a job sewing. She did that until she was married.

The public school was not a great force in Mrs. Greenbaum's life. She made an interesting contrast to her brother who graduated from Central High, went to college at the University of Kentucky, and graduated from medical school at Western Reserve University. The public school was part of his life.

The Greenbaums had one son. He, like his mother, worked with his hands. He graduated from East Tech High School which was a technical school at the time. Interestingly enough, she wanted him to go to college, but he had no desire to go. There are three grandchildren and all are college graduates. Mark is twenty-five and is a dentist in Cleveland. Cindy goes to law school at Emory University in Atlanta, Georgia. And Kim goes to Ohio State in teacher education. Mrs. Greenbaum added that neither granddaughter wants to come back to Cleveland.

David Spevack

When David Spevack was a year old, his father came to the United States. He had plans to bring the family as soon as he was settled. War broke out in Russia and it wasn't until he was eleven years old in 1923 that the family was able to join his father. The pogroms were suffered by Jews throughout Russia and Mr. Spevack's early years were spent running from place to place to avoid being captured. Needless to say, there was no school for Mr. Spevack in Russia. An agent sent by his father located the family at Odessa and brought them to the United States. Mr. Spevack's father was a tailor. Of course when the family came, his dad already spoke English. Yiddish was the language of the home, but everyone wanted to speak English. After a couple of years at school, Mr. Spevack remembers saying, "Mom, speak English, this is America." It was not one way for she was very eager to learn the language.

Mr. Spevack was put in kindergarten when he enrolled in grammar school. Even though he was eleven years old, the running and the scarcity of food during the pogroms left him the size of a six-year-old child. In grammar school, the teachers really wanted him to know English and they "put out" for him as a student. No one teacher stands out, but there was a pervasive feeling for learning between the kids and the teachers. The purpose was to learn English and "everyone" was working towards that end.

Mr. Spevack graduated from Glenville High School in 1932. School provided the knowledge that enabled him to enter the business world after graduation. Mathematics and English stand out as the most important subjects. Mr. Spevack wrote articles for the Glenville Torch, the school newspaper; he also sang in the choral club. Glenville was his school. He was accepted as one of its people and it was a comfortable place to go to school. Mr. Spevack recalls how proud his mom and dad were when he graduated from high school.

After graduation, Mr. Spevack got a job as a shipping clerk at a clothing house. He then had menswear and soft goods businesses.

In 1940 Mr. Spevack was married. He and Mrs. Spevack have three children. All are college graduates. One daughter graduated from Ohio State and lives with her husband in Cleveland. A second daughter and a son went to Ohio University and both live in California.

Mr. Spevack, reflecting, said that after Russia just being able to go to school was great.

Mrs. Wayne

It is very seldom that you meet someone whose strength and gentility is so evident. Mrs. Wayne is a very special person and I hope that this account can come close to doing her justice. Her family came from eastern Europe to London and then to the United States. Her schooling began in London and was completed in Cleveland. She was in England until she was eight years old. Mrs. Wayne's fondest memories of her schooling are from when she was still in England. She went to the Jewish Free School which was a primary school funded by the Rothchilds. The memories are all good ones. Learning and play were intermingled. There were middle class as well as poor children and the school was a place you felt comfortable in, you trusted, and you learned.

Mrs. Wayne was nine years old when she began school in Cleveland. It was in 1895. Since she had been to school in England, the language was never a problem. She remembers her accent being commented on numerous times. As for her schooling in this country, she felt that it was beneficial. At the same time, it was not as rigorous or warm as she and her family would have liked. She remembers her mother being very disappointed because the teachers did not seem to have the knowledge or compassion that the teachers had at the Jewish Free School in London. Mrs. Wayne stressed that school was not a bad experience. She went to three schools and each one had something that stood out as its own. Art and geography teachers are remembered as being excellent--each subject was enjoyed because of the teacher. One interesting rememberance was from Sterling School which was the second school Mrs. Wayne attended. She was the only white child in her class. Interestingly enough, the only anti-semitic memories are from the other two schools that she attended, Mayflower and Harmon schools. It was never a question of school being a bad place but it was very routine and ordinary. Mrs. Wayne did not go to high school. Her dad died and she had to go to work. She said that as a young girl her dream was college but that she knew it could never be anything but a dream. Only the very rich were college-bound at the turn of the century.

Mrs. Wayne got married when she was eighteen. The next ten-fifteen years of her life will show the faith she had in public education and education in general. When Mrs. Wayne got married, things were very rough

financially.   President   Theordore   Roosevelt   had
national job listings posted throughout the country.
It has to be remembered that although the Waynes were
not   extremely   orthodox,   they   did   have   traditional
Jewish ties (kosher, synagogue).   Although this was
true, they packed their bags and went where there was a
job: Valentine, Nebraska.   She and her husband and her
brother left for what reads as a real pioneer story.
Necessity was your teacher and some of the stories are
quite humorous as Mrs. Wayne tells them today.   Like
trying to explain to a butcher who never even heard the
word kosher what cut of meat you want and why.   She
said that she had a semi-kosher kitchen.

Pioneer or not, when it was time for the oldest
daughter to begin school, Mrs. Wayne decided it was
time for the family to move back to Cleveland.   The
one-room   schoolhouse   seemed   hardly   adequate   for   her
children.   There was one room for all grades.   College
seemed almost accessible and her kids were going to
high school.   All of Mrs. Wayne's children did graduate
from   high   school   and   two   children   graduated   from
college.   One son was in business; a second son is a
professor of art at Washington University in St. Louis.
One daughter works at the Jewish Community Center in
Cleveland.   Another daughter was a librarian and the
third was a music teacher.   All stayed in Cleveland
except   the   professor.   Grandchildren   are   spread
throughout North America.

The last sentence is interesting because it got
Mrs. Wayne talking about modern America.   About wanting
education and progress for her children and at the same
time suffering some of things you buy with progress.
Mrs. Wayne knows that you cannot go back, but also
knows that have made a different world.   "Man is just
not as important to his fellow man."

Sarah Gerson

    Mrs. Gerson came to Cleveland in the spring of
1904. She was eight years old when her family left
Russia. She had attended the Russian public school and
her memories were not pleasant ones. The family came
to America because her mother did not want Mrs.
Gerson's brothers to face conscription into the Russian
army. Ironically, one brother was drafted near the end
of World War I.

    Mrs. Gerson's dad was a cigarmaker when they first
came to Cleveland. Later he had a junkyard. Although
Yiddish was spoken in the home, there was never any
question about the children going to school. Mrs.
Gerson's dad had a concept of high school for his sons
and teacher school for his daughter. There was great
respect for the teacher. Mrs. Gerson remembers
teachers working very hard with her so that she would
learn English. Achievement was continually stressed by
both family and teachers. A great part of the language
was learned by mingling with other children. Also, she
remembers teachers having other children help her with
writing during class time.

    The teacher stood for America and since Mrs.
Gerson wanted to be an American the teacher was her
model. This, of course, goes back to the great respect
for teachers. Grammar was difficult for Mrs. Gerson
and it was her fifth grade teacher who pushed her. She
gave her a great deal of attention and helped her to
understand the English language. After that she
skipped to eighth grade which was her last year of
public school. Both Mrs. Gerson and one of her
brothers went to business school; her younger brother
graduated from high school. All the time Mrs. Gerson
went to school, she helped out in the family grocery
store. What is interesting is as great as the desire
was to be American, the language in the store was still
Yiddish. Old world ties were not severed quickly or
easily. Mrs. Gerson did clerical work until she was
married. Whether school had a direct effect in her
getting a job and her being able to do that job cannot
be answered. What she does know is that she could not
have got it if she had not mastered the English
language.

    Mr. Gerson went to high school and had a lumber
yard in Cleveland. They had two daughers who are both
married and live in Cleveland. Both graduated from

college, one from Ohio State and the other from Mather College of Case Western Reserve. There are also six grandchildren. A few of them are still in high school. Her grandson goes to Purdue. One granddaughter graduated from Ohio State and lives with her husband in Detroit. The other granddaughter graduated from Kenyon College and is a law student in Boston.

The public school was beneficial for Mrs. Gerson. It showed her the way to be an American. Obviously, the faith in education is not discarded in the following generations.

Mrs. Vendeland (Mr. Vendeland)

Mrs. Vendeland came to Cleveland from Austria-Hungary in 1914. She was eleven years old and the trip was made with her mother and sister. Her father and two brothers were already here. Her father had been for ten years and worked as a cement contractor. She had gone to school in Europe and was sent to school almost as soon as the family arrived in Cleveland. Her first experience with American public school was the "steamer class." Mrs. Vendeland came to Cleveland in June and was in this class from July until September when the regular term began. The teacher of the "steamer class", Miss Kelly, is the one teacher that sticks out in Mrs. Vendeland's school experience. Besides being her first contact with the American school, Mrs. Vendeland still finds her teaching remarkable. Somehow she was able to teach immigrant children English so that they could enter their chronological grade. In September Mrs. Vendeland entered the fifth grade. She says that she was not the exception, but rather Miss Kelly was that good. Mrs. Vendeland does not remember how she taught, but you knew English when you left her class.

In the home, school was seldom the topic of conversation. The family took in boarders, and dinner time and evenings meant political discussions. Although Yiddish was spoken, the conversation was American. She tried to speak English at home but the conversation usually came back to Yiddish. Of course school was never in question and she began fifth grade in the fall of 1914. Like Miss Kelly, the fifth grade teacher was especially dedicated. For the most part Mrs. Vendeland remembers her teachers as being committed to the learning of their students. No one teacher stood out again like Miss Kelly, yet all except one were encouraging and genuinely helpful. Mrs. Vendeland's grades were average. She did exceptionally well in spelling and grammar. Again we see the importance of language to the immigrant child. She said that it was in this strength that she found help as well as encouragement from her teachers. One teacher stands out as condescending and anti-semitic; that teacher leaves very few memories.

Mrs. Vendeland graduated from Longwood Grammar School and quit high school after tenth grade. She said that she was shy in school, but quitting had more to do with something at home rather than a school problem. The fact remains that she did quit and in later years felt the need to return for the education she felt she missed. She took courses in English at both Cleveland College and John Hay night school after she was married and had a family.

Mrs. Vendeland worked at a downtown Cleveland department store until she married Mr. Vendeland. When they got married she was twenty years old. Mr. Vendeland was almost six years her senior. American-born and one of twelve children, he graduated from Central High School. He got a job with a brokerage firm where he spent many years as a stockbroker. The Vendelands had four children. They lost one son in World War II. Their oldest daughter graduated from Glenville High. She is married to a certified public accountant and has four children. One of the Vendeland's grandsons is a graduate of Ohio State and is an accountant in Florida. The second grandson is a medical student at Case Western Reserve. One of the girls works in Denver and the other is a student at Ohio State.

The Vendeland's second daughter went to Cleveland Heights High School. She graduated from Mather College and taught school before she was married. Two of her children live in Israel and the third goes to Cleveland Hebrew Academy.

The youngest son went through junior high and works as a carpenter. His children went to high school and now work.

Mrs. Vendeland believes in education as evidenced by her returning to school. She felt that the public school was a good experience, but by no means the major force in her life. It certainly was not harmful.

Alex Gould

Mr. Gould came to Cleveland from Korompa, Hungary in 1910. He was ten years old and had been attending both public school and Hebrew school in Hungary. His mother brought his two sisters, his brother, and himself with her to the United States. Mr. Gould's father was already in this country when the family came. He had lived in Denver, Colorado and was stopping to see friends in Cleveland when his mother decided it was time to move the family to America. Mr. Gould remembers a great deal of discrimination in the Hungarian school. His mother had decided that there was no future for a Jew in Hungary. She sent a cable to America telling her husband not come back because she intended to join him.

Alex was the youngest child and he was taken to public school as soon as the family was settled. His dad had different jobs. The one Mr. Gould remembers was as a sweeper for six dollars a week. His mother lived for her children. Her goal was nothing less than professional status for Alex. Neither his mom or dad spoke English and learning the language was Mr. Gould's most difficult task in school. German was spoken in the home. Like many other children, he was put in the first grade even though he was eleven years old. Mr. Gould was in that class for a short time and then advanced rapidly. He really does not remember too much about particular teachers in grammar school. The thing that he does remember is his mother's great desire for him to get good grades and make it in school. She liked him to bring English home and she wanted to learn the language from her children. One incident that stands out is his mother coming to Longwood School to get him transferred. The school had a non-academic reputation and she was not going to have her son in a non-academic place. He was transferred to another school and he graduated from eighth grade when he was sixteen. Along with grammar school, Mr. Gould went to Hebrew school and had a Bar Mitzvah. He also went to shul on the sabbath until he began to work part-time.

After graduating from grammar school, Mr. Gould went to East Tech High School. He wanted to be a farmer and he got summer work, but his mother disapproved in no uncertain terms. The classic "what kind of job is that for my son" is what Mr. Gould remembers her saying. During high school he worked as a page at the public library, but his real interest was in mechanics. He enjoyed working on machines, and mechanics went along with math and English in his high school curriculum. ROTC was also part of Mr. Gould's high school studies.

For Mr. Gould the high school diploma was a ticket into the world of business. English helped him to communicate, math was essential, and his mechanic courses taught him how to work with tools and machines. He said that his mother really wanted him to be a dentist, but he was not interested. He was very close to going to dental school because she wanted it so badly. Mr. Gould ended up entering the hardware business. First he was a clerk and then he opened his own store. This store turned into a houseware manufacturing company which is now run by Mr. Gould's son-in-law.

This brings us to Mr. Gould's family. The Goulds have a daughter and son. Their home was kosher and they always belonged to a temple. Their children do not keep kosher homes, but they do belong to temples. Mr. Gould's daughter went to Ohio State for a year and then got married. She has two sons and a daughter. Both sons work for their father and live in Taiwan. The oldest is twenty-seven and went to Arizona State. The twenty-five-year-old graduated from Ohio State. Mr. Gould's granddaughter is a student at Ohio State. Mr. Gould's son went to Ohio University and graduated from Western Reserve. He has a married daughter who is twenty-three and lives in Cleveland. His twenty-one year old son works in his business and goes to night school at John Carroll. Mr. Gould's granddaughter is twelve years old.

School is looked back on as a second force after his mother. She was the force behind his going to school.

Faye Brooks

        Mrs. Brooks was born in Siberia. Her parent were
socialists and they had been sent to Siberia by the
government because of their political involvement. One
thing that she remembers is the comraderie between the
peasant and the political exile in Siberia. They
learned how to hunt and fish, and how to skin animals
to make clothing and rugs. She said they owed survival
to the peasant. Mrs. Brooks' father died and her
mother and stepfather brought her to the United States
in 1908. She was eight years old. The family settled
in Webster, Massachusetts. Her stepfather was a
shoemaker and there were many shoe factories along the
Massachusetts coast. Unlike most of the people I
interviewed, Mrs. Brooks' rememberances of the public
school are anything but good. There were two teachers
that were concerned and helpful, but the great part of
her experience is one of bigotry and anti-semitism. An
interesting aside is that Mrs. Brooks' younger sisters
did not meet with the same problems when the family
moved to Cleveland. Both graduated from high school
and one graduated from Western Reserve University. The
two teachers that Mrs. Brooks was fond of were her
kindergarten and fourth grade teachers. The
kindergarten teacher tried very hard to help her learn
English. She remembers her fourth grade teacher
because she made geography seen so real. The fourth
grade teacher was a person you could speak to and she
did not judge you on your nationality or religion.
Aside from these two teachers, Mrs. Brooks remembers
very hard times with both students and teachers. The
anti-semitism and the discrimination were a daily
affair. Her father and mother were both disappointed
because the hopes they had for their daughter were tied
to education. Mrs. Brooks said that she skipped school
many more times than she attended. Avoiding the truant
officer was a daily routine. When she was fourteen she
was expelled for fighting with a teacher. She said
that it was prompted by an anti-semitic slur. Her last
year of school was the fourth grade. Mrs. Brooks
worked in the shoe factory with her dad until the
family moved to Cleveland. Mrs. Brooks added that as
bad as school was, it could not kill her desire to be
an American.

        In 1919 Mrs. Brooks was married. Her husband,
also an immigrant, graduated from high school in
Conneticut. He worked as a truckdriver in Cleveland.
They had a son and a daughter. Both graduated from

high school, the son from East Tech and the daughter from John Hay. Mrs. Brooks' son has two daughters. One graduated from Kent and is married and lives in Cleveland. The younger girl graduated from the University of Cincinnati. She taught in Alaska and now teaches in Seattle, Washington. Mrs. Brooks' daughter has five children. There are four boys and a girl. One boy is still in high school and another attends the University of Illinois. Of the two other boys, one went to Ohio State and is a social worker in Cleveland, the other is a social worker in Jerusalem. Mrs. Brooks' granddaughter is a social worker in Wisconsin.

It is interesting that in spite of her experience, Mrs. Brooks still believes in the public school. She made sure that her children were not in the woods playing hooky like their mother.

Sarah Fich

Sarah Fich came with her family to Boston from Poland. She was nine years old and her folks sent her right to school. Her dad worked first as a peddler and then in a leather factory. Yiddish was spoken in the home, but her mom and dad stressed the importance of school for the children. The language and schoolwork came fairly easy for Mrs. Fich. She said that she could not recall any real problems. Most of the teachers were helpful and her sixth grade teacher stood out as exceptional. Penmanship was stressed in the early grades. Again, written communication was seen as essential for future work.

Mrs. Fich quit school when she was fifteen because she had to go to work. She worked at clerical jobs for which she said that her English training was essential. She did this kind of work until she got married. Mr. Fich had come to America from Odessa and went to school in this country. He became a pharmacist and they had a drugstore in Boston and then in New York.

The Fichs had two daughters and here is where we see that education is part of the family. One daughter who lives in Cleveland has an M.A. in speech therapy. Her husband is an engineer and they have two children. Their son has his degree from Princeton and his M.B.A. from Harvard. He is a business executive in Los Angeles. Their daughter is a social worker in Chicago. Mrs. Fich's other daughter, who lives in Great Neck, New York, has a doctorate in English literature and poetry. Her husband is a professor of physics. They also have two children. Their son graduated from Franklin and Marshall University and their daughter attends Swarthmore College.

Mrs. Fich thinks that the public school was good to both her husband and herself. She said that details are difficult to recall, but there was little harm and a lot of good. There is a tremendous faith in education that comes out when she talks about her daughters and her grandchildren and their education.

EDUCATION

GENERATION	GRAMMAR	HIGH SCH.	COLLEGE	GRADUATE
Immigrant-13	7	4	1	
Children-27	2	7	13	5
Grandchildren-35		3*	23	5

*4 still in high school

OCCUPATION

GENERATION	LABOR	BUSINESS	PROFESSIONAL
Immigrant-13	2	10	1
Children-27	3	14	10
Grandchildren-35		4	18*

*the rest are still in school

LOCATION*

GENERATION	CLEVELAND	OUTSIDE OF CLEVELAND
Immigrant-13	13	
Children-27	22	5
Grandchildren	19	16

*for grandchildren it is Cleveland or their parent's home.

Footnotes

[1]Studs Terkel, Hard Times (New York: Random House, 1970), p. 17.

[2]Richard Bartlett, "Some Thoughts After the Third National Colloquium on Oral History," Oral History (April, 1969), p. 271.

[3]Nathan Reingold, "A Critic Looks at Oral History," in The Fourth National Colloquium on Oral History, ed. by Gould P. Colman (New York: The Oral History Assn., 1970), p. 217.

[4]Ellul, The Political Illusion (New York: Alfred A. Knopf, Inc., 1967), p. 13.

[5]Ellie Abel, "A Working Reporter (and Unlicensed Practitioner) Looks at Oral History," in The Fourth National Colloquium on Oral History, ed. by Gould P. Colman (New York: The Oral History Assn., 1970), p. 27.

[6]Ibid.

[7]Saul Benison, "Reflections on Oral History," The American Archivist (January, 1965), p. 72.

[8]Donald Schippers, "The Literature of Oral History," in The Second National Colloquium on Oral History, ed. by Louis Starr (New York: The Oral History Assn., 1968), p. 37.

[9]William Leuchtenburg, "A Panel of Historians Discuss Oral History," in The Second National Colloquium on Oral History, ed. by Louis Starr (New York: The Oral History Assn., 1968), p. 4.

[10]Ibid., p. 6.

[11]Elizabeth Rumics, "Oral History: Defining the Term," Wilson Library Bulletin (March, 1966), p. 603.

[12]Benison, "Reflections on Oral History," p. 75.

[13]Henry Resnick, "When America Was Singing Buddy, Can You Spare A Dime?", Saturday Review (April 18, 1970), p. 30.

[14]Herbert Adolphous Miller, The School and the

Immigrant (Cleveland, Ohio: Cleveland Foundation, 1916).

CHAPTER 5

THE SEARCH FOR EDUCATIONAL ROOTS:
TRENDS IN THE SCHOOLING OF THE IMMIGRANTS

The division in history of education continues between those who defend the sanctity of the public school and those who view public education as an abomination. In many respects, it has become a religious issue for both sides. In A Critique of New Commonplaces, Jacques Ellul writes that there is little difference between ideologues of the left and ideologues of the right.[1] People and issues are no longer of concern, but rather the sustaining of one's ideological stand is all important. This dogmatism leads to limitless stands, and there is danger on both sides. On the one side, the schools are all good and do no harm, while the other side sees them as all evil.

Both Cubberley and the radical historians argue a highly partisan interpretation. Where Cubberley saw only the public schools beneficence, they see only its maleficence. Where Cubberley saw it as the symbol of American success, they see it as the symbol of American failure.[2]

For both sides, the school is an abstraction. Cubberley and the like are blind to human individuality, as well as the differences and the problems that existed within the school. The revisionists, on the other hand, choose to deny the many successes of the public school. Neither side chooses to involve itself with the historical reality of public education. Bernard Mehl analyzes that history:

In the end, for all his naivete, Cubberley is right--the compulsory school movement was part of the Puritan plan to keep sanity in a wilderness society, but enlarged to include every man. The Puritan error was in trying to substitute utopia for existence. The radical error comes when he tries to erase utopia from existence.[3]

Diane Ravtich, who is cited above, comes to the same conclusion as Professor Mehl. She is elated that modern education is finally free of the shallow history of Cubberley, but she then realizes that modern educational history is neither deep nor brings us

97

closer to an understanding of the public school:[4]

> ...historians select the passages and
> the quotes that make their case against
> American education and the liberal tradition.
> A history that is rich with controversy and
> complexity is reduced to a simple ideological
> line. The school is a failure, they tell us,
> without giving us a deeper understanding of
> what the schools have and have not
> accomplished.[5]

Although thirteen interviews with Jewish
immigrants who attended public school cannot give us a
definitive statement, they do help us begin to
understand how schooling affected the immigrant. The
trends that we see in these people's lives attend
directly to the questions posed in this study. Was the
public school good for the immigrant child or was it in
fact harmful? Are the "American dream" and melting pot
concepts myths or reality? And finally, how is the
alienation and fragmentation in modern day America
related to education?

The interviews show that those that take one
dogmatic stand or the other on the nature of the
influence of the schools really do not have ground to
stand on. The schools were neither great educational
utopias nor did they inflict harm on immigrant
children. There are incidents of discrimination and
condescension, but the greater part of the immigrant
experience in the public school was a good one.

There were a number of common denominators that
tied the immigrant to the public school. Being an
American was of utmost importance to both the children
and their parents. The obvious way to become American
was through the public school. This faith was
essential--the immigrant family felt that the school
had the ticket that would make the kids American. On
more than one occasion it was mentioned that the
teacher was a model of what was American. English and
mathematics were the major subjects. English, of
course, had to be stressed because knowing the language
was part of becoming American. There were special
classes for immigrant children in some schools. They
were called "steamer classes" and the people
interviewed still found it remarkable how quickly
English was learned in these classes. No one was sure
how the teacher taught them the language, but each said
that English came naturally after this short class. If

a school did not have a "steamer class", the immigrant child began in kindergarten or first grade. Progress was usually rapid and many times children were able to join their chronological grade within a year. Teachers are remembered as being tolerant and encouraging. Timothy Smith and Maxine Seller have both touched on this great desire that the immigrant children had to learn the language.[6]

The people interviewed in this study were no exception. It might be that it was this great desire as much as teaching or the school that facilitated learning the language. Taking this issue a step further, it might be that the immigrant children would not let the school fail:

> Quite as much as any coercion from compulsory education acts or any pressure from professional Americanizers, the immigrant's own hopes for his children account for the immense success of the public school system, particularly at the secondary level in drawing the mass of working class children into its embrace. By their presence, and by their commitment to these several ambitions, the first generation of immigrant children prompted educators, in administrative offices as well as classrooms, to a thousand pragmatic experiments geared to the interests and needs of their students.

It has to be remembered that more often than not the immigrant child was excluded from public school in Europe. His possibilities had been rather gloomy and America represented a new chance. Mom and dad worked in the sweatshop or as peddlers, but there was a bigger and better America that was open to the immigrant child. Whether the words of "American dream" or the Horatio Alger stories that were read in school were meant by the teacher or not does not really matter in the final analysis. What does matter is that the words were read and once they were spoken, they were digested by the immigrant. This can be observed in the great fear of southern whites at the thought of Blacks reading.[8] The following passage is taken from My Bondage and My Freedom by Frederick Douglass. It is the reaction of his master to him being taught English by his master's wife:

> Master Hugh was amazed at the simplicity of his spouse, and, probably for the first

time, he unfolded to her the true philosophy of slavery, and the peculiar rules necessary to be observed by masters and mistresses, in the management of their human chattels. Mr. Auls promptly forbade the continuance of her instruction; telling her, in the first place, that the thing itself was unlawful; that it was also unsafe, and could only lead to mischief. To use his own words, further, he said, 'if you give a nigger an inch, he will take an ell; he should know nothing but the will of his master, and learn to obey it. Learning would spoil the best nigger in the world; if you teach that nigger how to read the Bible, there will be no keeping him...If you learn him how to read, he'll want to know how to write; and this accomplished, he'll be running away with himself.'[9]

As it was for Frederick Douglass, language was very important for the immigrant. Reading and writing were keys to opportunity and equality.

Over and over again, penmanship is mentioned as a most important subject. We are told that teachers stressed it and that the children loved to write. One thing that we find is that reading and writing meant good-bye to the sweatshop. It meant a new kind of job where you could use the things you learned in school. It is easy now not to give credence to a job as a clerk or a receptionist; but for the immigrant woman, it was a step up. The factory was a thing of the past.

Becoming an American, the English language, and a better job all went together for the immigrant. It is almost as if it was unconscious; that is what happened in America. Very little is remembered about teaching technique or curriculum. The how could not be discussed. School was simply a place where you learned, and that learning prepared you for life in the new country. There are still questions to be asked, but it does not appear that the schools killed the spirit of immigrant children. To the contrary, it appears that the public school helped the immigrant child get what he wanted. And what he wanted was to be an American.

Of the thirteen people whose interviews are recorded, five graduated from high school and one from college. Two people quit in high school. One woman quit in the fourth grade and the remaining five people

graduated from grammar school (eighth grade). The
obvious question is that if the school was good for the
immigrant, why didn't he finish high school? But Mark
Krug reminds us that quitting school after eighth grade
was not unique to the immigrant.[10] In the early
twentieth century, this was thought of as a complete
education.[11] When someone said that they graduated
from school, they meant that they completed eighth
grade. According to Krug's figures, the percentage of
people that went to high school after grammar school
was less than those that attend college today.[12] Only
the very bright or the trade-oriented student went to
high school (or very rich).

Although the above is true, both Timothy Smith and
Diane Ravitch's statistics show that both school
success and social and economic mobility were greater
for the immigrant than for native born Americans. This
is from Smith's "Immigrant Social Aspirations and
American Education":

> Statistics for literacy and school
> attendance in the federal census of 1910
> suggest that immigrant families showed as
> much or more zeal for education as those in
> which the parents were native Americans. Not
> just in the south, where the school system
> was weak and the former slave population
> large, but in every section of the country,
> the percentage of children of foreign or
> mixed parentage aged six to fourteen who were
> enrolled in the school closely approximated
> that for children of native Americans. And
> the literacy of the immigrant's offspring was
> uniformly higher, even in the populous Middle
> Atlantic and North Central states, where
> newcomers from central and southern Europe
> were many, and traditions of education among
> the Yankee population strong.[13]

Professor Ravitch paraphrases Andrew Greeley on the
income mobility of the "new immigrant."

> Andrew Greeley reported recently that
> the descendants of what formerly were the
> most disadvantaged white minorities have
> surpassed the white Anglo-Saxon Protestant
> groups in terms of income. The highest
> average incomes were those of the Jews, Irish
> Catholics, Italian Catholics, German
> Catholics, and Polish Catholics in that

order.   Episcopalians and Presbyterians
followed the "new immigrant" groups on the
national income ladder.[14]

But now back to the schools; as I indicated above,
the grammar school education opened up worlds that the
Jewish immigrant could not have aspired to without it.
The second chapter quotes C. Wright Mills'
documentation of the prestige and glamour that a job in
an office meant to the immigrant.[15]   The Jewish
immigrants that were interviewed support Mills' thesis.
A job using the things you learned in school was a job
to be proud of.   In the preceding chapter, Mr. Lev
talked about his first job working as a clerk in an
office. Just by the inflection in his voice, you could
tell that he was proud that it was not as a street
peddler or sweatshop worker.   Some educational
historians argue that the preparation for the new white
collar jobs as well as learning a trade were tools used
by the public school to keep the immigrant in his
place.   Both Michael Katz and Colin Greer make this
argument, but the lives of the immigrants do not
support their thesis.

Of the thirteen people interviewed, one woman
worked in a factory and another woman sewed until they
were married.   The other eleven never saw the factory
or the sweatshop where their parents toiled.   One man
graduated from college and was a teacher and
businessman. Two other men were businessmen. And the
rest of the women were either secretaries,
receptionists, or clerks.   It can be said that it is no
great story, unless you realize what their folks did
for a living and also what life was like in Europe.
The people interviewed repeatedly spoke of being unable
to attend school in Europe. In some cases, it was the
reason given for leaving.   In the Pale your movement
was restricted to certain areas and there was strict
control over the types of jobs available for Jews.

Another question that has validity is what about
people that did not go to school and made it? Doesn't
that prove that school was not necessary? The issue,
though, was not the necessity, but rather the
opportunity the schools provided. Those immigrants who
wanted the offerings of the public school were helped
in their quest by the public school. If the immigrant
wanted to make it in school, he could do just that.
The issue is made clearer in Michael Harrington's The
Other America. Harrington tells us that since everyone
was poor, there was room for the immigrant to "bust

102

out." For Harrington, that was the reality of the early twentieth century, but not the reality of today. The school was an "opener" because the society was open. But no longer is the school an opener because society is no longer open.[16] Again, Professor Ravitch makes the same point in The Revisionists Revised. She speaks of upward mobility for the immigrant fifty years ago that has changed to a rigid class structure for Blacks and Puerto Ricans in 1977.[17] It is in this bond that the immigrant had with America that the public school gathered its strength. The public school was good for immigrant children because society was open and the children and their parents would not let this opportunity elude them.

Indeed, turn-of-the-century Jewish parents on the lower east side of New York City nearly rioted when their children were not admitted to public schools because of overcrowding, and immigrant parents throughout the city voted out of office a mayor who tried to introduce reforms into their public schools in 1917.[18]

These findings do not mean that the criticism of the public school during immigrant times is all unfounded. There was bad teaching and there was archaic methodology. But it was still a place where teachers had to teach children because the children and their parents demanded learning. Mr. Lev's English teacher, Miss Adams, and Mrs. Vendeland's first teacher, Miss Kelly, exemplify the possibility of teacher meeting student in the public school. It supports the thesis of the book Teacher by Sylvia Ashton-Warner. Miss Ashton-Warner went to teach Maori children and the success rate was magnificent. At first she attributed the success to methodology. However, when that methodology was called upon again and could not be recaptured, she realized it was more a case of her and the children, of teacher and student.[19] "When I teach people, I marry them."[20] This is the way she described teaching and it is not far from the descriptions given in some of the interviews.[21]

The immigrant believed that the public school was his ticket to the "American dream", and he made sure it was that ticket. He did easier and better paying work than his father, and his children would move up even further. The faith in education became even stronger. Twenty-seven children are mentioned by the people interviewed. Of those twenty-seven, fifteen graduated

103

from college. All but two graduated from high school.
Professors, doctors, teachers, social workers, an
engineer, and businesmen are occupations of this second
generation. The faith in education remained and with
the extension of schooling came the broadening of
occupational possibilities. But as possibilities and
options open up, with them come new issues. The
children of the people interviewed were already
different than their moms and dads, just as their moms
and dads differed from their parents. Religious and
family activities were just not as important for the
children as other things began to occupy time--school,
politics, and business, just to name a few. Kosher
homes and synagogue attendance were less frequent for
the second generation than they were for their folks.
And a few people moved out of town because that is
where jobs could be found. This trend becomes much
clearer with their children.

The faith in education has not lessened, but
education has become perfunctory, rather than
meaningful, as it was for the immigrant. Not to go to
college is very strange, college is something an "in"
class does. In a sense, calling education a religious
experience for the immigrant is not in error. Although
it was a ticket and was the beginning of the twentieth
century American ethos, it was also something that was
infused with meaning. If he was less Jewish, the
immigrant replaced Religion with being an American.
For his children this lessened and for his
grandchildren there does not seem to be anything
binding. Only three of the grandchildren did not go to
college and those that graduated are spread throughout
North America. A great percentage are professional
people, but the telling figure is how many live in a
different city than their parents.

Nineteen of the thirty-five grandchildren have
settled away from their homes. Many reasons are
given--jobs, opportunities, adventure, etc.--but one
thing that is apparent is that roots, whether they be
family or educational, are not part of the modern
college graduate. Although the immigrant left
tradition to become American, he still had a sense of
commitment and roots. His new commitment was being an
American and that meant trade offs but not sell outs.
For his grandchildren there are no sell outs either,
but only because there is not commitment in the first
place. The public school and the university are no
longer important because they are a gift and not even
an appreciated one at that. Along with dispersion

104

throughout the land comes even lessened religious ties. Sartre talks about the intellectual Jew in Anti-Semite and Jew.²² Although he is talking about France, he describes the American Jew perfectly. Why be too Jewish when it just gets in the way? This, though, is not the case of only the Jew, rather the above seems symptomatic of modern man. Commitment, loyalty, and roots only stand in the way of progress. A twenty-three year old girl from Cleveland could not teach school in Seattle, Washington if she was tied to her mom and dad, or if they were tied to her. The answer, of course, is that we live in another age. Or do we?

One interesting trend that became clear in the interviews is that a number of the third generation are reaching back for their religious roots. The numbers were not great, but even if there was only one, it would still be significant. Two families had two children in Israel and two families had a child in the Hebrew Academy. Obviously it is not a Jewish renaissance, but it still seems to point to a searching for roots in an impersonal, atomized world. The Lubavich movement in Judaism, the Hari Krishnas, etc. are a sign of tremendous alienation and fragmentation, just as is the popularization and probable ethnic reproductions of Alex Haley's Roots. And although there is a tremendous danger of demagoguery, a number of Jewish kids coming back to Judaism is a sign that they are not exponents of a lonely world. It is a sign that alienation and fragmentation have limits even though we seek a limitless existence. When Alex Haley's book catches on as it did, it might be that people want commitment and loyalty and roots. Unfortunately, as good as Roots is, geneological studies do not bring spiritual roots to an alienated world. And all the family trees that are done because of the book do not bring man closer to man. The hope is that we can transcend roots as an abstraction and look deeply into our common human condition where our spiritual roots lie.

As we trace the journey of the people interviewed, we study a group of people that came to America with great aspirations. Their folks did manual labor and sent them to school so that they would never have to do the same kind of work. They worked in business and sent their children to school with even higher aspirations. The hope was that the children would either expand the business or have a profession. The hope became reality and for the next generation--my generation--college was assumed. The "American dream" and "melting pot" are not myth, but rather reality for the Jewish immigrant.

But for the Jewish immigrant there was a price that came with the "American dream". Each generation has become less Jewish and the importance of family roots has lessened as families find themselves dispersed throughout the country. In this dispersion we find ourselves atomized and man no longer communes with his fellow man. It is hard to get a hold on something because nothing is lasting and binding. At the same time, people are searching for something substantial. They are looking for their historical roots. It is in this search for something substantial, it is in this search for historical roots, that I now turn back to the public school.

Albert North Whitehead and John Dewey have written about teaching as a religious experience and for the Jewish immigrants interviewed, the school was this religious experience. Along with the practical aspects, of which they were well aware, there was a spiritual reality to the public school. Learning the language and the American dream were so vital for the immigrant that the school had tremendous meaning. At the same time, the school was infused with energy from the commitment and loyalty the immigrant brought with him. The relationship was a symbiotic one that was energized by the involvement the immigrant had with the school.

The grandchildren of the immigrants do not have this relationship with the public school. The credentials are accepted, but energizing ideas are neither brought in nor pulled out by this generation. There is very little personal involvement and the schools are now in question.

The infusion of energy into American education means opening up the public school to a new force. In a world where alienation and fragmentation seem to be rule rather than exception, the commitment and loyalty of the old Jewish family looks more and more inviting. But that is now a lost culture. If the public school is to become a vital force, it has to open up its doors to Blacks. And not just in numbers, but rather in an honest acceptance of the Black man into the American ethos. The aspirations the Jewish immigrant mother had for her children, the "American dream", college, and a good job, are the words of the Black mother today. The

106

same energizing force the Jewish immigrant brought to the schools when they emigrated from Europe will be revitalized if we honestly open up the American school for the Black man as we did for the Jewish immigrant at the turn of the century.

Footnotes

[1]Ellul, <u>A Critique of New Commonplaces</u> (New York: Alfred Knopf, 1968), pp. 215-220.

[2]Ravitch, <u>The Revisionists Revised</u>, p. 11

[3]Mehl, "Who's Liberated," p. 397.

[4]Ravitch, <u>The Revisionists Revised</u>, p. 70.

[5]<u>Ibid.</u>

[6]See Timothy Smith and Maxine Seller, Chapter 3 of this paper. Their essays are "Immigrant Social Aspirations and American Education" and "The Education of Immigrant Children in Buffalo, New York, 1890-1916."

[7]Smith, "Immigrant Social Aspirations and American Education," p. 250.

[8]Frederick Douglass, <u>My Bondage and My Freedom</u> (New YorK: Dover Inc., 1969), pp. 145-146.

[9]<u>Ibid.</u>

[10]Krug, <u>The Melting of the Ethnics</u>, pp. 85-86.

[11]<u>Ibid.</u>

[12]<u>Ibid.</u>, pp. 86-95.

[13]Smith, "Immigrant Social Aspirations and American Education," pp. 236-237.

[14]Ravitch, <u>The Revisionists Revised</u>, pp. 26-27.

[15]Mills, <u>White Collar</u>, p. xiii.

[16]Michael Harrington, <u>The Other America</u> (New York: Macmillan Co., 1964), pp. 4-5.

[17]Ravitch, <u>The Revisionists Revised</u>, p. 24.

[18]<u>Ibid.</u>, p. 19.

[19]Sylvia Ashton-Warner, <u>Teacher</u> (New York: Simon and Schuster, 1963), pp. 25-26.

[20]Ibid., p. 209.

[21]See the interviews in Chapter 4 with Rae Davis and Nathan Lev.

[22]Sartre, _Anti-Semite and Jew_, pp. 130-153.

BIBLIOGRAPHY

Books

Addams, Jane. <u>Democracy and Social Ethics</u>. New York:
The Macmillan Co., 1907.

Antin, Mary. <u>The Promised Land</u>. Boston: Houghton-
Mifflin Co., 1969.

Arrowhead, Charles. <u>Thomas Jefferson and Education in
a Republic</u>. New York: McGraw-Hill, 1938.

Ashton-Warner, Sylvia. <u>Teacher</u>. New York: Simon and
Schuster, 1973.

Barton, H. Arnold. <u>Letters from the Promised Land</u>.
Minneapolis, Minnesota: University of Minnesota
Press, 1975.

Buber, Martin. <u>I and Thou</u>. New York: Charles
Scribner's Sons, 1967.

Cahan, Abraham. <u>The Education of Abraham of Cahan</u>.
Philadelphia: The Jewish Publication Society of
America, 1969.

_____. <u>The Rise of David Levinsky</u>. New York:
Harper and Brothers, 1917.

Callahan, Raymond. <u>Education and the Cult of
Efficiency</u>. Chicago: University of Chicago Press,
1962.

Cash, W. J. <u>The Mind of the South</u>. New York: Alfred
A. Knopf, 1941.

Chandler, B. J.; Stiles, Lindley; and Kituse, John.
<u>Education in Urban Society</u>. New York: Dodd, Mead
and Co., 1962.

Church, Robert, and Sedlak, Michael. <u>Education in the
United States</u>. New York: The Free Press, 1976.

Cooley, Charles Horton. <u>Human Nature and the Social
Order</u>. New York: Schocken Books, 1964.

Covello, Leonard. <u>The Heart Is the Teacher</u>. New York:
McGraw-Hill, 1958.

Cremin, Lawrence. <u>The Genius of American Education</u>.

Pittsburgh: University of Pittsburgh Press, 1965.

_____. The Transformation of the School. New York: Alfred A. Knopf, 1961.

Curti, Merle. The Roots of American Loyalty. New York: Russell and Russell, 1946.

Cubberley, Ellwood. Changing Conceptions of Education. Boston: Houghton-Mifflin Co., 1909.

Daniels, John. America Via the Neighborhood. New York: Harper and Brothers, 1920.

Dewey, John. Democracy and Education. New York: The Macmillan Co., 1963.

_____. The School and Society. Chicago: The University of Chicago Press, 1943.

Douglass, Frederick. My Bondage and My Freedom. New York: Dover Publications Inc., 1969.

Dubois, W. E. Burghardt. Dusk of Dawn. New York: Schocken Books, 1940.

_____. The Souls of Black Folk. New York: Blue Heron Press, 1953.

Ellul, Jacques. A Critique of the New Commonplaces. New York: Alfred A. Knopf, 1968.

_____. The Political Illusion. New York: Alfred A. Knopf, 1967.

_____. The Technological Society. New York: Alfred A. Knopf, 1967.

Fuchs, Lawrence. American Ethnic Politics. New York: Harper and Row, 1968.

Glazer, Nathan, and Maynihan, Daniel Patrick. Beyond the Melting Pot. Cambridge, Mass.: The MIT Press, 1970.

Goldman, Eric. Rendezvous With Destiny. New York: Alfred A. Knopf, 1956.

Goodman, Paul. Growing Up Absurd. New York: Random House, 1956.

Greer, Colin. The Great School Legend. New York: Basic Books, 1972.

Haley, Alex. Roots. New York: Doubleday and Co., 1976.

Handlin, Oscar. Immigration as a Factor in American History. Englewood Cliffs, New Jersey: Prentice-Hall Inc., 1959.

_____. Race and Nationality in American Life. Boston: Little, Brown and Co., 1948.

_____. The Uprooted. Boston: Little, Brown and Co., 1951.

Harrington, Michael. The Other America. New York: The Macmillan Co., 1964.

Haskin, Frederic. The Immigrant. New York: Fleming H. Revell, 1913.

Herberg, Will. Protestant--Catholic--Jew. Garden City, New York: Doubleday and Co., 1955.

Hofstadter, Richard. Social Darwinism in American Thought. New York: George Braziller, 1955.

Howe, Irving. World of Our Fathers. New York: Harcourt Brace Jovanovich, 1976.

Hutchinson, E. P. Immigrants and Their Children, 1850-1950. New York: John Wiley and Sons Inc., 1956.

Itzkoff, Seymour. Cultural Pluralism and American Education. Scranton, Pennsylvania: International Textbook, 1969.

Jefferson, Thomas. The Complete Thomas Jefferson. New York: Tudor Publishing Co., 1943.

Josephson, Mary, and Josephson, Lester. Man Alone. New York: Dell, 1962.

Kallen, Horace. Cultural Pluralism and the American Idea. Philadelphia: University of Pennsylvania Press, 1956.

Karier, Clarence; Violas, Paul; and Spring, Joel. Roots of Crisis: American Education in the

Twentieth Century. Chicago: Rand McNally and Co., 1973.

Katz, Michael. Class, Bureaucracy, and Schools. New York: Praeger Publishers, 1971.

_____. Education in American History. New York: Praeger Publishers, 1973.

_____. School Reform: Past and Present. Boston: Little, Brown and Co., 1971.

Kierkegaard, Soren. The Present Age. New York: Harper and Row, 1962.

Krug, Mark. The Melting of the Ethnics. Bloomington, Indiana: Phi Delta Kappa Educational Foundation, 1976.

Levi, Carlos. Christ Stopped at Eboli. New York: Farrar, Strauss and Giroux, 1947.

Lubell, Samuel. The Future of American Politics. New York: Harper and Brothers, 1951.

Mann, Horace. Lectures on Education. Boston: Ide and Cutton, 1855.

Mannheim, Karl. Ideology and Utopia. New York: International Library of Psychology, 1936.

Maxwell, William. A Quarter Century of Public School Development. New York: American Book Co., 1912.

Mayer, Martin. The Schools. Garden City, New York: Doubleday and Co., 1961.

Mehl, Bernard. Classic Educational Ideas: From Sumeria to America. Columbus, Ohio: Merrill, 1972.

Mills, C. Wright. Power, Politics, and People. New York: Ballantine Books, 1963.

_____. White Collar. New York: Oxford University Press, 1956.

Nevins, Allan. Allan Nevins on History. New York: Charles Scribner's Sons, 1975.

_____. The Gateway to History. New York: D. C.

Heath and Co., 1938.

Nietzche, Friedrich. The Gay Science. New York: Vintage, 1974.

Novak, Michael. The Rise of the Unmeltable Ethnics. New York: The Macmillan Co., 1971.

Perkinson, Henry. The Imperfect Panacea. New York: Random House, 1968.

Puzo, Mario. The Fortunate Pilgrim. New York: Lancer Books, 1964.

Ravitch, Diane. The Great School Wars. New York: Basic Books, 1974.

_____. The Revisionists Revised: Studies in the Historiography of American Education. Syracuse, New York: National Academy of Education, 1977.

Riis, Jacob. How the Other Half Lives. New York: Hill and Wang, 1957.

Ross, Edward. Changing America. New York: Century Press, 1912.

_____. Sin and Society. New York: Houghton-Mifflin, 1907.

Sanders, Ronald. The Downtown Jews. New York: Harper and Row, 1969.

Sartre, Jean Paul. Anti-Semite and Jew. New York: Schocken Books, 1948.

Schrag, Peter. The Decline of the Wasp. New York: Simon and Schuster, 1971.

Schulberg, Budd. What Makes Sammy Run. New York: Random House, 1941.

Sennett, Richard. The Uses of Disorder. New York: Alfred A. Knopf, 1970.

Singer, Isaac Bashevis. In My Father's Court. New York: Farrar, Straus and Giroux, 1962.

Stephenson, George. A History of American Immigration. New York: Ginn and Co., 1926.

Terkel, Studs. Hard Times. New York: Avon Books, 1972.

_____. Working. New York: Pantheon Books, 1972.

Thompson, Frank. Schooling of the Immigrant. New York: Harper and Brothers, 1920.

Tyack, David. Turning Points in American Educational History. Waltham, Mass.: Blaisdell Publishing Co., 1967.

Ward, Frank. Dynamic Sociology. Vol. I. New York: Appleton, 1924.

Welter, Rush. Popular Education and Democratic Thought in America. New York: Columbia University Press, 1962.

Whitehead, Albert North. Adventures of Ideas. New York: The Macmillan Co., 1933.

Zierold, Norman. The Moguls. New York: Coward McCann Inc., 1969.

Dissertations

Herold, Jeffrey. "The American Faith in the Schools as an Agency of Progress: Promise and Fulfillment." Unpublished Ph.D. dissertation, The Ohio State University, 1969.

Nelson, Richard. "The Pathological Model and the Schools: A Critical Inquiry." Unpublished Ph.D. dissertation, The Ohio State University, 1975.

Periodicals

Abel, Ellie. "A Working Reporter (and Unlicensed Practitioner) Looks at Oral History." The Fourth National Colloquium on Oral History, 1969. Edited by Gould P. Colman. New York: The Oral History Association, 1970.

Bartlett, Richard. "Some Thoughts After the Third National Colloquium on Oral History." Journal of Library History 4 (April, 1969), 169-172.

Barton, Judy, and Moorer, Frank. "A Report on Oral

History at the Martin Luther King Jr. Memorial Center." Journal of Library History 7 (January, 1972), 61-63.

Benison, Saul. "Reflections on Oral History." The American Archivist 28 (January, 1965), 71-77.

Leuchtenburg, William. "A Panel of Historians Discuss Oral History." The Second National Colloquium on Oral History, 1967. Edited by Louis Starr. New York: The Oral History Association, 1968, pp. 1-7.

Mehl, Bernard. "Who's Liberated." The Review of Education, Vol. 2 (July/August, 1976), 391-399.

Reingold, Nathan. "A Critic Looks at Oral History." The Fourth National Colloquium on Oral History, 1969. Edited by Gould P. Colman. New York: The Oral History Association, 1970, pp. 213-227.

Resnick, H. S. "When America Was Singing Buddy, Can You Spare A Dime?" Saturday Review 53 (April 18, 1970), 27-30.

Rumics, Elizabeth. "Oral History: Defining the Term." Wilson Library Bulletin 40 (March, 1966), 602-605.

Schippers, Donald. "The Literature of Oral History." The Second National Colloquium on Oral History, 1967. Edited by Louis Starr. New York: The Oral History Association, 1968, pp. 33-40.

Seller, Maxine. "The Education of Immigrant Children in Buffalo, New York: 1890-1916." New York History LVII/2 (April, 1976).

White, Helen. "Thoughts on Oral History." The American Archivist 20 (January, 1957), 19-30.